BEFORE YOU READ HOMER

THE GODS, HEROES, AND MYTHS YOU NEED TO KNOW

Brett Robbins

APORIA
PRESS

APORIA
PRESS

First Aporia Press Edition 2015

ISBN-10: 0-692-49320-4
ISBN-13: 978-0-692-49320-5

Printed in the United States of America

10 9 8 7 6 5 4 3 2 1

THANKS TO MOM AND DAD
SIMPLY, MY BEST FRIENDS

CONTENTS

"Homer and Hesiod were the first to compose Theogonies, and give the gods their epithets, to allot them their several offices and occupations, and describe their forms." Herodotus

"Both Homer and Hesiod have attributed to the gods all things that are shameful and a reproach among mankind: theft, adultery, and mutual deception." Xenophanes

INTRODUCTION

You spend ten years teaching a subject and little by little you whittle away what's most superfluous about each topic you cover. The first few years you dutifully report on Heracles' minor labors, as though comprehensiveness were the ultimate goal. But it isn't. Not for me at least. The first few years you throw in everything but the kitchen sink but gradually some things float to the surface and demand greater attention. You surrender to the allure of depth, preserving as much breadth as necessary to give students a good overview of the terrain without patronizing them by treating them as though they'll never think about myth again after taking the Final.

Throughout the writing of this book I constantly had one not-the-least-bit-rhetorical question in mind: "So what?" I find that too many introductions to myth rehash the same facts already covered sufficiently by Edith Hamilton in her 1942 classic *Mythology*. There's an unspoken rule that, like translations of Homer, every generation must have their mythology primer. This is nonsense. Hamilton's primary sources are for the most part also our own. Coming later does not guarantee being better, and in the case of mythology primers I have found that the authors of the best ones are motivated first and foremost by a fascination with the primary sources and a passion for looking at them anew.

That's what I try to do in this book. It takes you on a short journey—a weekend cruise, if you will—through ancient Greek myth, leading you up to Homer's doorstep. It proceeds chronologically but it's not dominated by chronology. It's important to know when events occur but mainly in relation to one another, not because the numbers are themselves important. We'll be stopping off at the ports I find most intriguing, primarily from the standpoint of how myth informs various aspects of Greek culture.[1] Many more trips remain to be taken, however, and this book is intended to be a launch-pad for your own.[2]

The ancient Greeks lived in a world before the Internet, before airplanes, before trains, before the telegraph. They had only myths to transmit through writing and images on vases and sculptures and buildings. Myths were their only mode of transportation and communication combined. There were no TVs, no newspapers. Just traveling bards singing songs so enthralling that their myths were absorbed by the bloodstream unconsciously, as the collective assumptions of society. Sometimes words and images were used to try to explain things, sometimes they served the interests of those who commissioned them to be propagated.

How did everyone in Greece know to worship Zeus and Heracles? *Myths*. Myth linked otherwise disparate communities through the shared currency of the Greek language. Myth is a fungible cultural technology: its ability to be disseminated via various artistic media made it the most feasible way for distant *poleis* to communicate with each other in something like the way we do more efficiently today via the mass media. The myths, then, had to captivate their audiences as quickly and powerfully as possible. Hence the sensationalistic imagery they inspired, the outrageous actions perpetrated by larger-than-life characters. It all seemed so outlandish, so unrealistic, so overtly fictional. And yet, Theseus was both a king and a hero, Zeus was both a god and a king. There was overlap between these worlds. And there still is today.

---

[1] The Greeks were in turn influenced by the Egyptians and Mesopotamians. In the first two chapters, then, we'll deal with one central myth from each of these two civilizations.

[2] Please note (rather than merely footnote) the conspicuous lack of the word "All" in this book's subtitle. I realize that the "The" might seem to imply "(all of) The," but that's not my intention. If the "The" implies anything it's "The Gods, Heroes, and Myths (I Think) You Need to Know." Which in turn is based on my own bias about what aspects of myth I think it's necessary to know about before delving into Homer: the Olympian gods and the four most important Greek heroes leading up to the Trojan War. I leave out much more than I include. This is neither a confession nor an apology but simply the result of the culling process referred to above.

CHAPTER ONE

NARMER

Egypt was the first state in the world to be brought under the control of one person, the first pharaoh Narmer, who convinced his people to unify Upper and Lower Egypt so they would be stronger than they were apart. And how did he achieve this? Through a *myth*. In this chapter we're going to look at the myth he used to persuade his people to pool their resources rather than continue to fight against each other. Egypt didn't exist in a vacuum any more than Greece did. So although a book on the Greeks might be expected to begin with the Greeks, it's a mistake to disregard the rest of the Mediterranean area, the trade that went on there with other states, and the potential for conflict that convinced Narmer of the wisdom of unifying Egypt in the first place.

The myth in question is used for the purpose of propaganda. But not all myths are, as we'll see when we get to the Greek creation myth, which has a proto-scientific function, to help explain the universe. The Greeks used myths as propaganda too, however, and we'll get to Greece soon. But the myth we're going to look at now originated in Heliopolis and spread both to Hierakonpolis, where Narmer was from, and to Nagada, which was at war with Hierakonpolis and against unification.

Keep in mind that whether or not two or more regions should unify into a sovereign state is not always a no-brainer. There's debate about whether or not it should happen, as in Germany in the early 1990s when Nobel Prize-winning author Günter Grass argued, against the grain of public opinion, that if East and West Germany were to unite it would create more problems than solutions. But this is even more so in the *ancient* world, when it's not so easy to unify people, to make them feel as though they all belong to the same community. This is the kind of thing we take in stride today because transportation and communication are so much quicker and more efficient. It's a much smaller world now than it was when both travel and communication were done by foot, by

3

horse if you were lucky, never by machine.

When you live in a world like that it's in the best interest of whoever's in charge to get everyone on the same page, so they think: "We are Egyptians" or "We are Greeks." That's a big deal, something not to take for granted. The Founding Fathers of the US didn't take it for granted. How could the members of the different colonies become unified, get to the point where they thought of themselves as belonging to a single community? It wouldn't happen on its own. You have to get them to think of themselves less as colonists and more as Americans. This is precisely the same sort of challenge Narmer confronted in his attempt to sway public opinion toward everyone thinking of themselves as Egyptians. Narmer knows that his own region, Hierakonpolis, is on the Horus team and that the region he has to win over, Nagada, is on the Seth team. So he circulates a story in which Horus prevails over Seth and lets the symbolism percolate throughout society rather than try to coerce them with orders that will only inflame them.

It's debatable whether Narmer himself came up with this myth or appropriated it for the purpose of convincing the Egyptians to unify. Some say it was too perfectly tailored to its historical context not to have been invented for it from whole cloth, others that it must predate Narmer, but no one knows for sure.[3] What we do know is that Narmer knew that in Hierakonpolis the god Horus was worshipped and in Nagada Seth was worshipped and that the most effective way he could convey his message without merely telling his subjects what to do or explaining to them why they should do it was to propagate the Horus-Seth meme.

The *Heliopolis Creation Myth* begins with Nun, the infinite ocean, and from Nun springs a giant mound of dirt called Benben, and on Benben lives the sun-god Atum, signifying that out of the formless mass

---

[3] That's not surprising, however, any more than it is, say, that no one knows how writing came back into the picture at the beginning of Greek history after disappearing at the end of Greek *pre*history. One scholar claims it was an adaptation of the script used by the Mycenaeans, another that it was invented for the sake of preserving Homeric epic, and so on. Who are these scholars? Let's not get bogged down in secondary sources in this book. Let's listen to the primary sources themselves. My next book will be packed with footnotes and secondary sources because it will be an attempt to prove that Homer invented cinema.

of Nun, gods and people eventually need a place to live. So Benben emerges, which is inspired by a structure first conceived of as a stairway to heaven:

Atum would rather not live alone on Benben, so he gives birth, on his own, to two deities: Shu, god of air, and Tefnut, goddess of water. Shu and Tefnut mate and they give birth to Geb, god of earth, and Nut, goddess of sky.[4]

Already at the beginning of the universe, then, the four elements are accounted for: fire (Atum), air (Shu), water (Tefnut), and earth (Geb).[5] Shu and Tefnut are conventional twins, Geb and Nut are conjoined twins. Atum is jealous of Geb and Nut for being connected the way they are, while he himself doesn't have anyone he's close to at all, having given birth alone to beings who from then on would get to mate to have children.[6] Once Atum separates Geb and Nut, Nut is portrayed as arching over Geb, who is lying flat on the ground, ithyphallically, symbolizing

---

[4] In *Greek* mythology, on the other hand, the counterpart to Geb (Gaea) is female and the counterpart to Nut (Uranus) is male, a disparity consistent with the opinion of Herodotus that: **The Egyptians, in agreement with their climate, which is unlike any other, and with the [Nile] river, which shows a nature different from all other rivers, established for themselves manners and customs in a way opposite to other men in almost all matters.**

[5] This notion of the four elements being the basic stuff of the universe is adopted by the earliest Greek philosophers as well.

[6] Notice we're already getting into the concepts of unity and disunity.

that by mating each night (her body touching his causes the darkness) they generate the rest of the universe:

Now that Atum has opportunistically separated Geb and Nut, each day at dawn he enters through Nut's fingers, shines his sun throughout the day onto the earth below him along the trajectory of Nut's arching body, descends into the Underworld at dusk through her toes, and emerges through Nut's fingers again each morning to perpetuate the cycle. Geb and Nut give birth to four deities: Osiris, Isis, Seth, and Nephthys. Osiris marries Isis, Seth marries Nephthys. Osiris becomes king of Egypt and Seth is jealous. *The drama commences.*

Just as Atum was jealous of the intimacy of Geb and Nut, so Seth is jealous of Osiris being the ruler of the gods. So he captures Osiris, locks him in a chest, and throws it into the Nile.[7] Seth usurps Osiris' throne. Then we get the fairytale-like detail of the chest drifting out to sea and washing up on shore, where a tree envelops it with its branches and leaves until Isis (who has been searching all over the world for her husband[8]) finally finds the chest he's been locked in, opens it up, and discovers that he's already dead. She transforms herself into a bird and flaps her wings to resuscitate him. They have sex one last time and produce the falcon god Horus, depicted here in a family photo:

---

[7] We'll see the locking-in-a-chest motif again in the story of Perseus.
[8] This detail will be echoed thousands of years later in the story of Demeter, goddess of grain and psychotropic flowers.

[9] Seth finds Osiris' corpse and chops it up into several pieces, all but one of which Isis finds and reassembles so Osiris can live again. The absence of his penis, however, disqualifies him from ever again having children or, by extension, ruling Egypt, requiring Horus to step into the breach and usurp his throne. Osiris, no longer the pharaoh, becomes god of the dead, a kind of Egyptian Hades, although whereas Hades will be hated because of his Underworld credentials, Osiris remains, along with Horus, one of the most respected gods of the Ennead,[10] not in spite of but rather because of living in the Underworld.[11]

The symbolism employed by Narmer in the myth we just looked at is much simpler than the myth itself: Horus, its hero, is the god who endures in this struggle we just witnessed. The message from Narmer is,[12] "Worshippers of Seth: we're the guys who worship Horus and we're telling you that if we all unify with Horus as our standard bearer, we'll beat whatever potential enemy might come our way, no matter how powerful."

---

[9] All images in this book are part of the public domain. I refrain from labeling them by artist, provenance, etc. because my reason for using them, for the most part (the next image being an exception), is to illustrate my points in a way that could be served by any number of examples of the same motif rather than only by a given work in particular.

[10] The fancy name given to the first nine Egyptian gods.

[11] In Egyptian mythology the afterlife is depicted more positively than its Greek counterpart, consistent with the real-world practice of mummifying the pharaoh so he can live on forever, along with his retainers and daily items he'll need once he completes his journey. The giant walls of the interior of the pyramid are covered with hieroglyphs, detailed instructions for the voyage ahead. They are intended for no one's eyes but the pharaoh's, in stark contrast to our own times when creating art is often a means to the end of attaching one's name to it and exhibiting it to the public.

[12] I will be engaging in my share of Thucydidean "quoting" throughout this book, the verbal equivalent of how I'll be using images. The idea is the thing.

Behold the Narmer Palette:

On its front (left), Narmer is depicted at home (symbolized by a close-up) wearing the headdress of Upper Egypt. On its back (right), he's depicted far away from home (symbolized by a long shot) wearing the headdress of Lower Egypt.[13] The Palette, then, commemorates the unification of Upper and Lower Egypt, the mythical lion-type figures with elongated necks representing the intermingling of north and south, the achievement propagandized in the *Heliopolis Creation Myth*.[14]

---

[13] Perhaps you're wondering why I don't put quotation marks around such apparent anachronisms as "close-up" and "long shot" when dealing with a civilization that predated film by fifty centuries. Because film and cinema are not synonymous. We don't need to use shame-quotes when attributing to ancient art stylistic techniques shared by pictorial, verbal, and filmic cinema.

[14] The circular area formed by the intertwining necks—the focal point of the back of the palette—is where the cosmetics go.

CHAPTER TWO

GILGAMESH

We now turn to a myth from the Near East, which deals with the afterlife in a much different way than the *Heliopolis Creation Myth*. The *Epic of Gilgamesh* is the earliest extant epic poem of world literature, featuring the first hero as well. His story comes from Mesopotamia, the land between two rivers, the Fertile Crescent, the Cradle of Civilization. The primary focus of this story is not on the afterlife *per se* but on life on earth, the suffering resulting from knowing we have to die, its alleviation through the acceptance of our mortality. That's not to say Mesopotamia wasn't a theocracy as well. It was. It even had its counterpart to the Egyptian pyramid, the ziggurat:

Gilgamesh is the first "flawed hero," exhibiting the sort of imperfections we encounter later in the anthropomorphic gods of the Olympian pantheon. He is a Sumerian king and he's two-thirds divine, more than a demigod but not all the way a god, which matters because in our story he's going to try to become a god through and through and we're going to see what happens because of it.

Gilgamesh starts out as a harsh, merciless king but ultimately becomes more humble through the lessons he learns.[15] At the beginning of the story he is accused by the gods of hubris, of thinking of himself as something more than mortal. And why not? He's two-thirds divine after all. But the gods want him to know he's not one of them, not all the way a god, which makes all the difference.[16] So they punish him by sending a wild mountain man named Enkidu to kill him:[17]

Enkidu descends from the mountains and challenges Gilgamesh to a fight. So far all you've had is a haughty king and the gods being mad at him. Now there's a wrench in the works, a James Bond villain sent to kill him and we wonder what he's going to do next. If he fights Enkidu in hand-to-hand combat he will certainly lose (which is why the gods sent him in the first place).

Gilgamesh, however, is more an Athena than an Ares,[18] more brains than brawn:[19] instead of fighting Enkidu he visits Shamhat, the temple prostitute, and sends her to Enkidu to seduce him, to symbolically tame the wild-man. They have sex for seven days and seven nights until Enkidu becomes mellowed out and, from the look of this selfie, quite the lady's man:

---

[15] His character grows, in other words. Although the *Epic of Gilgamesh* is the first extant epic in world literature, it's by no means merely an Ur-epic that will eventually be supplanted by more complex and interesting epics in the future. It is quite simply one of the greatest epics of all time, period.

[16] This will be a recurrent dilemma for Greek heroes as well.

[17] Enkidu is the first beast-like human being in world literature, who symbolizes wildness, lack of culture, in short, the opposite of a respectable man, let alone a hero. The man-beast duality will come into play perhaps more than any other throughout this book.

[18] If you don't know what I mean by that, savor your not knowing it the way you do a meal that has just been placed in front of you. I say this not only about this particular contrast between Ares and Athena but in a more general sense as well: the joy of learning is born out of curiosity, and rather than get frustrated by what you don't know yet, get excited by the prospect of learning about it later.

[19] This is a thumbnail summary of their differences that will make more sense later.

Before long Enkidu and Shamhat have a little relationship going on, and Enkidu, suddenly remembering why he's been sent from the mountains in the first place, can't be bothered with it any longer. He's happy now and everything's great. He and Gilgamesh become buddies. Now it's a road movie. They team up to fight and kill the giant Humbaba sent down to them by the gods as punishment for having had so much fun.[20] Ishtar (the Sumerian equivalent to Isis and Aphrodite) falls in lust with Gilgamesh, who rejects her.[21] The gods send another creature against Gilgamesh, the Bull of Heaven, the third monster sent against him.[22] He and Enkidu kill it as well, which symbolizes the defeat of culture over wildness, of human over beast, and that through Shamhat's magical touch Enkidu has been transformed from a wild beast to enough of a man for his teaming up with Gilgamesh against a wild creature to possess legitimate man-against-beast symbolic significance:

The gods punish Gilgamesh by killing Enkidu. Notice the irony here: first they send him down to kill Gilgamesh, then they punish Gilgamesh by killing the guy who has been sent down to kill him but is now his best friend. Gilgamesh is so distraught by Enkidu's death (anticipating Achilles and Patroclus) that he sets out to find out how to revive Enkidu (as Isis did for Osiris)

---

[20] The "generation gap" takes root: the old resents the ways of the young out of envy for no longer being the young that is resented by the old.

[21] It's worth pointing out that when we hear about characters in myth who barely if at all know each other falling in "love" with each other, it's almost always a euphemism for lust.

[22] A bull will also be sent to Minos, founder of Minoan civilization (as we'll see in the THESEUS chapter), but it will be from the sea rather than the sky and benign rather than malignant. The Minoans traded extensively with Egypt; such correspondences are not coincidental.

and, while he's at it, to discover the secret of immortality in a more general sense. To do so he takes a long journey by boat to the other end of the universe, embarking on the first hero-quest in world literature:

 Gilgamesh travels to the far reaches of the earth and visits his relative Utnapishtim to ask him how to revive Enkidu and become immortal himself. He finds out, however, that such things are impossible for mere mortals. "I have good news for you, though" says Utnapishtim, "There's a plant I know of that can keep you young for as long as you live."

Gilgamesh is excited by this prospect and goes to much trouble to procure some of the plant from the bottom of the sea. On his way home, however, he puts it on the ground to go bathe in a river and while he's gone a snake slithers up to it and eats it, thereby robbing Gilgamesh of lifelong youth and vouchsafing it for himself (that's why it sheds its skin). At first this depresses Gilgamesh greatly, but then he comes to terms with this turn of events, realizing that although he has to eventually die, he's not entirely obsolete after all, for he has the power to determine what kind of king he'll be in the future, so that the memories others have of him will live on in a good way rather than a bad way.

CHAPTER THREE

URANUS, CRONUS

The movie "Troy" leads us to believe that the gods don't play much of a role in the lives of Greek heroes in Homer. In the *Iliad* itself, however, the centrality of the gods becomes immediately apparent:

SING, goddess, the anger of Peleus' son Achilles
and its devastation, which put pains thousandfold upon the Achaeans,
hurled in their multitudes to the house of Hades strong souls
of heroes, but gave their bodies to be the delicate feasting
of dogs, of all birds, and the will of Zeus was accomplished
since that time when first there stood in division of conflict
Atreus' son the lord of men and brilliant Achilles.[23]

Already in the first five lines we meet the Muse of epic poetry (line 1) and Zeus (line 5), who transmits to her the story Homer asks her to sing. And that's just the beginning: the Olympian gods and goddesses intervene constantly throughout the epic, are indeed essential to it, the divine machinery that drives it forward. Which is why, in the next six chapters, we'll be focusing on the world of the gods taken for granted by Homer's audience as the cosmic backdrop of his epics, which are themselves the cultural backdrop of ancient Greece and Rome.

In the *Iliad,* whose events begin *in medias res* in the tenth year of the Trojan War, Homer presupposes in his audience an acquaintance with Zeus, king of the gods, Athena, goddess of war, Hermes, god of heraldry, and so on. But where do these divinities come from? Enter Hesiod, a contemporary of Homer, author of the *Theogony*, a narrative poem that, while shorter than either the *Iliad* or the *Odyssey*, is no less influential, including as it does the first Greek systematic account of the origins of the universe and an explanation for how Zeus becomes king of

---

[23] All translations in this book, unless otherwise noted, are by Richmond Lattimore. His translations, especially of Homer, have still not been improved on, despite the home-court advantage of subsequent translators who base their authority on the misconception that each generation should necessarily scrap the translations of the previous ones, as though coming later necessarily meant being better.

the gods in Olympus. In this sense, Hesiod's poem is the Greek counterpart to the *Heliopolis Creation Myth*.

At the beginning is Chaos, Greek counterpart to Egyptian Nun. It's not an ocean, however, but a void, a lack of anything at all. So while the Greek word "chaos" has been imported into English, it means something different from what the Greeks meant by it at first, an empty space to be filled up later with the things that come into being. Chaos, by itself, produces five primordial deities (recalling Nun and Benben): Gaea ("Earth"), Tartarus (as close as the Greeks come to Hell), Eros ("Lust"[24]), Erebos ("Darkness"), and Nyx ("Night," which underscores the soon-remedied fact that at this point we still don't have its opposite).

If you travel to Greece you'll notice that the sea and mountains and sky are its most dominant geographical features.[25] It's not surprising, then, that from Gaea alone emerge the first three manifestations of nature that meant (and still mean) the most to the Greeks: Pontus ("Sea"), Ourea ("Mountains"), and Uranus ("Sky"). Gaea and Uranus mate with each other through their *hieros gamos* ("sacred marriage," when Uranus rains onto Gaea), and six Titans and six Titanesses are conceived. Hyperion (a Titan) and Theia (a Titaness) will give birth to Helios ("Sun"), Selene ("Moon"), and Eos ("Dawn"). Iapetus (a Titan) will sire Prometheus ("Forethought"), foremost champion of human beings. Mnemosyne ("Memory") will bear the Muses, who inspire artists to creation. Rather than go over the rest of the Titans (and their children, and their children's children, which could easily fill up an entire book),[26] the two we will focus on next are Cronus ("Cutter"[27]) and Rhea ("Flow"), who will get things going dramatically.

---

[24] See footnote 21.

[25] It's because of its extremely mountainous terrain that so many isolated communities sprang up throughout Greece and, as a corollary, that it was so difficult for Greeks from different *poleis* to gain a sense of belonging to an all-encompassing political entity. Panhellenic cultural festivals were designed to mitigate this sense of fragmentation (or rather, non-integration), as were the natural language of Greek and the cultural language of myth. Then again, until the Macedonians came into the picture (think the Federalists), the Greeks were quite content with the localism of their political structure (think the anti-Federalists).

[26] Or to engage in more elegant variation on the theme of giving birth.

[27] His very name requires a spoiler alert.

Before the Titans are born, the *Theogony* is primarily a Creation Myth, dealing with the beginning of the universe. Now it turns into a Succession Myth, dealing with the three stages leading up to Zeus becoming king of the gods in Olympus. Stage One begins when Gaea is still pregnant with her children but Uranus, king of the universe, informed by an oracle that one of his children will usurp his throne, prevents them from being born by pushing down on their heads as they try to emerge from Gaea. Gaea, then, in terrible pain from this treatment, invents the sickle and says to her yet-unborn children, "One of you must stand up against your father and keep him from preventing you from being born." Cronos is the only one to rise to the occasion (literally) and take the sickle into his hands. And when Uranus tries to have sex with Gaea, Cronos castrates him:

Once Uranus is castrated, Cronos takes his genitals and throws them over his shoulder. Once they hit the ground they produce the Giants ("Earthlings") and Hecatonchires ("Hundred-Handers"). The genitals keep rolling along the ground until they reach the sea and plunge into it and from the surface of the sea emerges a fountain of foam and from it the goddess Aphrodite ("Foam-Given"):

Aphrodite, then, is the first of the Olympians. We now begin Stage Two of the Succession Myth, with Cronus as the new king of the universe. Cronus has the same problem as his father, however: he too hears that one day one of *his* kids will usurp *his* throne. So what does *he* do about it? When Rhea is pregnant with a bunch of children, each time one of them springs from her womb (rather than from the earth, as with Gaea) Cronus swallows it:

Cronus swallows[28] one kid after another and Rhea goes back to her parents and asks them what to do about her terrible predicament. "Okay," they say, "you have one more kid you haven't given birth to yet, don't you?" "Yes," she says. "Take him to the island of Crete and give birth to him there." "But what happens when Cronus demands that I give him the final child?" asks Rhea. "Disguise a stone as a baby," says Gaea, "by wrapping it in swaddling clothes and hand it to him."

Cronus takes the stone and swallows it, vomiting up all his kids, the first generation of Olympians.[29] The Titanomachy ("Titan-Battle") ensues between the Titans and the Olympians. The Olympians win, Zeus becomes king, and the third and final stage of the Succession Myth is complete.

---

[28] Rather than chews up, as in the (too) famous (not to include) Goya painting above. Here, as with the Botticelli on the previous page, with its PC shell, we have another artist taking liberties with the facts provided by the literary sources. Rather than knock him for it, however, we should see what he's doing in the light of sampling, mash-ups, tributes, and other types of creative appropriation of the works of others so prevalent today.

[29] Namely, Hestia, Demeter, Hera, Hades, Poseidon, and Zeus. Hestia will begin as an Olympian but eventually be replaced by Dionysus. Hades, for reasons given later, is not considered to be one of the Olympian gods. This chapter ends with the birth of another Olympian. Thus, not counting Hestia and Hades, Hesiod's *Theogony* accounts for the first six of the twelve canonical Olympians. We'll deal with the identity and nature of the Olympians in their own respective chapters.

Zeus marries Metis ("Mind") and finds out what Uranus and Cronus found out: that his throne is in danger of being usurped. So what does *he* do? Obviously it will be a different sort of solution than the ones adopted by Uranus and Cronus, given the fact that Zeus manages to hang onto *his* throne.[30] How does he do it? Rather than swallow his children, as Cronus did in vain, he swallows *Metis herself* while she's still pregnant, to prevent her from delivering their child. Before long, however, Zeus starts experiencing pain in his head from all the pressure caused by the child needing to emerge from it (recalling Gaea when Uranus prevented her from giving birth to the Titans, or a *Dermatobia hominis*). Hephaestus,[31] the craftsman god, then, cuts open the top of Zeus' head and from it springs Athena, the goddess of war and wisdom, in full armor:

---

[30] We only know this retrospectively, however. Should we allow ourselves such heuristic latitude?

[31] There are two versions of Hephaestus' birth. One says he's the son of Zeus and Hera, the other that Hera has had him alone. The painting above, then, presupposes the parthenogenous origin of Hephaestus. This is as good a time as any to point out that there exist several different, often conflicting, variations for many of the myths treated in this book. Rather than attempt something relatively comprehensive like what H.J. Rose achieves in his *Handbook of Greek Mythology*, I have limited myself either to the one version of a given myth thought to be most authoritative by general consent or, short of that, to data shared by two or more versions considered to be equally (or at least comparably) authoritative.

CHAPTER FOUR

ZEUS, HERA

Zeus (Roman: Jupiter) is now the king of Olympus, and that's the mythic backdrop for nearly every story there is, from Homer onwards.[32] After the Titanomachy there is a lottery between the victors that determines who will be in charge of which regions of the universe. Zeus is allotted the most coveted region of all: the sky. Poseidon is allotted dominion over the sea.[33] And Hades is allotted the least desirable region of all, the Underworld, where he'll live and rule for eternity, at first quite lonely but eventually allowed to marry his niece Persephone.

Unlike king Agamemnon, who will lead the Greeks during the Trojan War despite Achilles being the intrinsically superior warrior, Zeus not only rules over the other Olympians but he's also by far the strongest Olympian as well, made clear by Homer in a passage in the *Iliad* in which he asserts his dominance by informing his siblings and children[34] that if he wished to he could beat them all at tug of war:

'Come, you gods, make this endeavor, that you all may learn this.
Let down out of the sky a cord of gold; lay hold of it
all you who are gods and all who are goddesses, yet not
even so can you drag down Zeus from the sky to the ground, not
Zeus the high lord of counsel, though you try until you grow weary.

---

[32] What we'll do in the next four chapters, then, is deal with the Olympian deities themselves, one at a time (Apollo), two at a time (Zeus, Hera; Demeter, Dionysus), and seven at a time (Aphrodite, Ares, Hephaestus, Athena, Poseidon, Hermes, Artemis [I don't include Hestia in this list because she's not one of the twelve canonical Olympians]). Then we'll devote a chapter to Hades before moving onto the Greek heroes for the rest of the book (except for the APPENDIX, which gets into language).

[33] Which really means the sea *and* the earth, although we normally associate Poseidon with the sea because it's his digs. Yet there seems to be more to it than that: that the Greeks could consistently refer to a god presiding over both sea and earth (most conspicuously in the form of earthquakes and floods) as the "sea-god" is (as with the identity of Gaea's first children), a reflection of the centrality of the sea to Greek culture. A visit to Greece today corroborates that, indeed, some things never change.

[34] According to a different mythic tradition than the one represented by Hesiod's *Theogony*, Aphrodite is the daughter of Zeus and the oracular deity Dione. Tradition has it that Homer and Hesiod competed in a poetry contest at some point in their lives. One wonders if they disputed about things like this.

Yet whenever I might strongly be minded to pull you,
I could drag you up, earth and all and sea and all with you,
then fetch the golden rope about the horn of Olympus
and make it fast, so that all once more should dangle in mid air.

Olympus eventually means something like what later cultures will mean by "Heaven," but starts out exclusively as the tallest mountain in Greece, far up in the north, bordering Thessaly and Macedonia. Homer gives Zeus the epithet "Cloud-Gatherer," reflecting the fact that as sky-god he is in charge of thunder and lightning, the celestial counterpart to Poseidon's floods and earthquakes. Consistent with his function as sky-god, Zeus' most conspicuous attribute is the thunderbolt. His bird is the eagle. So when you see either or both of these symbols in Greek art, it will most likely be a picture of Zeus:

Zeus has several different roles as king of the gods, with their corresponding titles. One of his titles, *Olympios*, is ambiguous because it refers to either of two roles: as king of the gods in Olympus or as patron god of Olympia, one of the main religious shrines in ancient Greece and site of the fifth-century-BC Temple of Zeus at Olympia (472-456 BC):

Within the temple was housed one of the seven wonders of the world, a 43-foot-tall statue of Zeus made of gold and ivory, which no longer exists. If you visit the site of the temple today, here's what you will find:

Fortunately, however, much of the sculpture from the Temple of Zeus has been preserved. Take another look at the picture of the temple above. The triangular area just below the roof is called a pediment, and within each pediment at either end of the temple the artist we refer to as the "Olympia Master" sculpted two self-contained narratives.

Here is the extant sculpture from the east pediment of the Temple of Zeus at Olympia:

It depicts the moment of calm before a chariot race presided over by Zeus (center), between a king named Oenomaos (to Zeus' right) and Pelops, a suitor of his daughter (to Zeus' left). Oenomaos has learned from an oracle that he's destined to be killed by his son-in-law.[35] Thus he prevents all suitors of his daughter from marrying her by challenging them to a chariot race with the ultimate stakes: if they lose they die. Already eighteen suitors have challenged Oenomaos and all of them have died. He's that good. What, then, can Pelops do?

We'll get to that in a minute. First we need to understand that the Temple of Zeus is situated within the same sacred shrine to Zeus as the Olympic stadium. Just as Athenian drama was performed in the Theater of Dionysus, within a religious context, so were the Olympics performed, with the same attention to ritual as drama, in the Olympic Stadium at the shrine of Zeus. And while the Theater of Dionysus is located in close proximity to the Parthenon (Athena's main temple on the Acropolis), so the Olympic stadium is located in close proximity to the Temple of Zeus:

The squarish area at the bottom center of the photo is called the Leonidaion, and it's where the athletes lived while they competed in the Olympic Games. Within the smaller squarish (albeit more rounded) area at the top right of the photo, that long rectangular strip of land extending through it, like the line through a circular "No" sign but without touching the edges, is the Olympic stadium.

---

[35] Sound familiar? This motif will start ringing even more bells once we get into the hero chapters.

Right between the Leonidaion and the stadium is the Temple of Zeus with the pedimental sculpture featuring the chariot race between Pelops and Oenomaus facing east, toward the stadium. And finally, right next to the Temple of Zeus, also between the Leonidaion and the stadium, is the Hippodrome, where the horse-racing event at the Olympics occurred, close enough to Zeus' temple that he can watch the athletes compete.

Pelops, then, decides that he has to cheat by bribing Oenomaos' charioteer Myrtilus: if he replaces the metal linchpins of the king's chariot with wax ones, he'll let Myrtilus sleep with his new wife. Myrtilus agrees, Oenomaos is killed, and Pelops wins the race. When Myrtilus comes to collect, however, Pelops betrays him by throwing him off a cliff. On his way down to the water, Myrtilus curses Pelops, initiating the infamous curse of the House of Atreus (Atreus is Pelops' son) that we'll get into in the AFTER TROY chapter.

These kinds of associations between characters from different parts of Greece (i.e., Pelops being cursed so that his son's son will suffer tragic consequences a hundred miles away in Mycenae) are a way for the Greeks to produce the illusion that the various *poleis* of Greece all inhere within a single overarching cultural continuum. Narmer used the symbolism of the *Heliopolis Creation Myth* to propagandize the unification of Egypt in a less heavy-handed way than simply to force Upper and Lower Egypt to unite.

In the sculpture of the east pediment of the Temple of Zeus, the Olympia Master is doing something different than that: rather than tell a story that implies: "It's better to unite our different parts so we can be stronger," here the Greeks are saying: "Pelops is in this chariot race and you know how it will end up. He will betray Myrtilus, who will initiate the curse of the House of Atreus, which of course you know about." In this case, then, the Olympians (from Olympia, that is, not to be confused with the other ones) don't merely symbolize how desirable it *would be* for Greece to unite but take for granted that Greece is *already united* through a shared mythic tradition.

The lyric poet Pindar, most famous for his songs commemorating victories by athletes in the various Panhellenic ("All-Greek")[36] Games, was quite aware of the crucial centralizing function he performed as one of the head PR men of Olympia (and, by extension, Greece), spreading the gospel of Zeus (and, by extension, myth):

Nor shall we sing games greater than the Olympian.
From there the manifold song is spread
by the skill of poets, to celebrate
the son of Kronos.

It is interesting to note how strategically centripetal the four Panhellenic venues are, facilitating a centralization of culture analogous to what the three main TV networks used to manage to achieve in the US:[37]

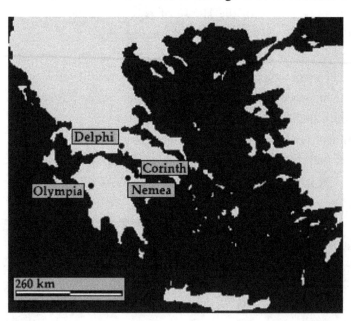

---

[36] In the sense of both the games being held all over Greece and being competed in only by Greeks.

[37] And to some extent still achieve, although their online nemeses Google, Facebook, Twitter, Instagram, etc. give them a run for their money.

Here is the extant sculpture from the west pediment of the Temple of Zeus at Olympia:

It depicts a wedding attended by centaurs who get fresh with the women and are vanquished by several men called Lapiths, aided by the Minotaur-slayer Theseus. The god in the middle may be Apollo (as usually supposed) or a younger version of Zeus.[38] To his left is Theseus, about to strike a centaur with his axe:

We clearly have an example of the culture-over-wildness theme we encountered with Gilgamesh and Enkidu in the *Epic of Gilgamesh*. And yet while the half-man, half-horse centaur, by virtue of his beastly nature, might seem a logical victim of elitist targeting by the indigenous hero of Athens, we will see that the four Greek heroes we'll be paying most attention to in subsequent chapters—Perseus, Heracles, Theseus, and Jason—all have something in common with Achilles (depicted in the following painting) that might surprise you: they were all at one point or another tutored by Chiron, the wise, sophisticated, compassionate, all-too-human being who, alas, also happened to be a centaur:

---

[38] An interpretation that allows us to compare the two situations Zeus finds himself in in the two pediments, an intriguing prospect.

The horse part is at the bottom, the human part is at the top. This is significant. Unlike the Minotaur—which is also half human and half beast (bull rather than horse), although the human part is the body and the beast part is the head—a centaur has a human head (and Chiron even has human arms), symbolizing his capacity for wisdom, which in Chiron's case is borne out by an especially impressive pedagogical resume. Are you getting the sense that the ancient Greeks had a tremendous capacity for, and love of, paradox?

As the sister and wife of Zeus, many of the stories Hera (Roman: Juno) has a role in tend to be in one way or another linked to the sky god, and frequently they involve her anger toward him for going behind her back with the male or female, mortal or immortal lovers he seduces by disguising himself as a human being or animal or cloud or shower of gold. She punishes him for it and leaves all kinds of destruction in her wake. If she goes too far, however, she pays the price, as we see at the end of Book 1 of the *Iliad* when she sees Zeus consorting with Thetis, mother of Achilles, and expresses confusion about what she sees (which, come to think of it, does look kind of suspicious):

Zeus will have none of it, however, as he tries to make clear to her:

'Hera, do not go on hoping that you will hear all my thoughts,
since these will be too hard for you, though you are my wife.
Any thought that it is right for you to listen to, no one
neither man nor any immortal shall hear it before you.
But anything that apart from the rest of the gods I wish to
plan, do not always question each detail nor probe me.'

26

At first Zeus is unsuccessful, receiving from Hera the sort of reply more appropriate to a wife who expects to be treated as an equal by her husband:

'Now, though, I am terribly afraid you were won over
by Thetis the silver-footed, the daughter of the sea's ancient.'

This doesn't last long, however, as Zeus takes things up a notch and threatens Hera with bodily harm:

'Dear lady, I never escape you, you are always full of suspicion.
But go then, sit down in silence, and do as I tell you,
for fear all the gods, as many as are on Olympus, can do nothing
if I come close and lay my unconquerable hands upon you.'

This scene is echoed at the end of *The Godfather*, when crime boss Michael Corleone's wife Kate insists on knowing whether or not he murdered his sister's husband and he reacts to her question much as Zeus does. Only, while Kate gets her way "this one time" (well, not really: he lies to her), Hera, predictably, does not:

He spoke, and the goddess the ox-eyed lady Hera was frightened.
and went and sat down in silence wrenching her heart to obedience.

To compensate for her constant invalidation by Zeus, however, Hera will project her anger frequently, not on Zeus himself, which is too dangerous, but on the children of Zeus born of mothers other than herself, the most famous and (not least because of the etymology of his name) conspicuous being Heracles.

CHAPTER FIVE

APHRODITE, ARES, HEPHAESTUS, ATHENA
POSEIDON, HESTIA, HERMES, ARTEMIS

Aphrodite (Roman: Venus), you'll remember, sprang up from foam in the sea once Uranus' genitals had been lopped off by Cronus with the sickle invented by Gaea for the purpose. She's the goddess of lust, not love, the Olympian embodiment of the primordial entity Eros, underscored by the fact that Eros (Roman: Cupid), the boy who flies around with a bow and arrow and shoots people to make them fall in lust with each other, often hangs out with Aphrodite and is shown doing so in much Greek and Roman (and subsequent) art:

This Eros has the same name as the other one but they're somewhat different: whereas the Eros to the left has the sort of dynamic personality one would expect from a companion of Aphrodite, his cosmic counterpart has no personality at all. Besides being the lust goddess, Aphrodite is also, predictably, notoriously unfaithful to her husband Hephaestus (Roman: Vulcan), the craftsman god (think *Beauty and the Beast*), whom she nevertheless sincerely loves despite being made fun of by the rest of the Olympians for being married to a god whose mother, Hera, threw him out of Olympus as soon as he was born because of how ugly she found him to be. Eventually, however, Hephaestus gets his revenge on Hera and is readmitted to Olympus.

When Aphrodite cheats, she most often does so, again predictably, with the war god Ares (Roman: Mars), son of Zeus and Hera, the "bad boy" of the Olympians. In a famous scene in the *Iliad*, however, Ares and Aphrodite both learn first-hand that although Hephaestus is a nice guy most of the time, he's by no means a pushover. Granted, he is the lame god, whom everyone makes fun of because of how he walks, talks, and looks:

Thereafter beginning from the left he poured drinks for the other
gods, dipping up from the mixing bowl the sweet nectar.
But among the blessed immortals uncontrollable laughter
went up as they saw Hephaistos bustling about the palace.

On this occasion, though, he is informed by Helios ("Sun"), who sees all, that his wife is carrying on an affair with Ares. So he builds a trick-bed that traps the two of them in it the next time they have sex and the rest of the Olympians surround the spectacle and laugh at them:

The first thing to associate with Athena (Roman: Minerva) is war, and in particular its strategic aspects, as opposed to Ares who glories in killing for its own sake and is thus, like Hades (but for different reasons) much hated by most of the other Olympians. The second quality to associate with Athena is wisdom, which complements the first quality: if there didn't have to be war, she would be the happiest of all.[39] Athena, however, is also the goddess of wisdom in a *general* sense, unlike Zeus

---

[39] Keep in mind, however, that Athena is usually referred to simply as the "goddess of war," despite her profound differences from Ares, even as Aphrodite is usually referred to even more inaccurately as the "goddess of love."

who, although the god of justice, is rarely referred to as wise: he's just too much of a cut-up, too fallible and adulterous to be thought of in the same exalted light as Athena, who is pretty much all business all the time. Athena's chief attributes are the owl (associated with wisdom), the spear and helmet she was born with, and sometimes her shield, gifted to her by Zeus. The origin of the shield goes back to the story of the goat Amalthea, who raised Zeus on Crete after he had been sent there by Rhea to prevent him from suffering the same fate from Cronus as his elder siblings. After raising Zeus, however, Amalthea was sacrificed to the gods and it was her skin that was used for the shield, called the *aegis* ("goat-skin [shield]"). The shield contains a snaky-haired head on it, belonging to none other than the Gorgon Medusa, placed there by the hero Perseus, son of Zeus, after he slays her.

The main attribute of Poseidon (Roman: Neptune) is his trident, a three-pronged fishing spear that, along with his beard (which he has in common with Zeus), is the go-to shorthand for artists to use to make it clear who is being depicted in a given painting or sculpture:

What is the first thing that comes to mind, however, when you hear the name "Poseidon"? The sea, of course, reflecting his function as the sea god. As for potential confusion between Zeus and Apollo based on their both having beards, we have no worry there, right? After all, Zeus is as well-known for his thunderbolt as Poseidon is for his trident. Confusion can only result from the thunderbolt or trident *missing*, right? And how likely is that to happen? Well, since you asked, a statue was found just off the coast of a town called Artemisium on the island of Euboea (the second-largest in Greece). The statue is called "Artemisium Zeus" or "Artemisium Poseidon," depending on whether you think he's holding a thunderbolt or a trident:

The place we normally associate with Athena is, of course, Athens, of which she is the patron goddess. She earned that distinction by winning a contest against Poseidon. Each deity needed to create something to woo the Athenians enough to induce them to make him or her their patron deity. Poseidon struck his trident into the ground on the Acropolis and a fresh-water spring came gushing forth from it. What could possibly be more impressive than that? Athena needed to come up with something more memorable, more symbolically compelling, so she created an olive tree—which gives us some idea of the importance of olives and olive oil to the Greeks and others around the Mediterranean—a moment commemorated on a pediment of the Parthenon:

Unfortunately there's not much to say about Hestia (Roman: Vesta). She was born to Cronus and Rhea along with Zeus and his siblings but isn't considered to be one of the twelve canonical Olympians. She was eventually replaced by Dionysus because they needed to spice things up in Olympus and who could possibly compete in that regard with the god of wine? Certainly not Hestia, the goddess of the fireplace. We've accounted so far, then, for seven of the twelve canonical Olympians: Zeus, Hera, Aphrodite, Ares, Hephaestus, Athena, and Poseidon. Aphrodite is born before the four[40] born to Cronus and Rhea and then Athena comes along later. Hera and Zeus give birth to Hephaestus and Ares, husband and lover of Aphrodite, respectively.[41] The rest enter the picture as offspring of Zeus.

The birth of Hermes (Roman: Mercury) to Zeus and the sea-nymph Maia is featured in a work called the *Homeric Hymn to Hermes*. The Homeric Hymns were named after Homer but not composed by him. They were named that way because in style and theme they were thought to be Homer-*like*. The *Homeric Hymn to Hermes* dramatizes how within an hour of his birth the eponymous god went and stole the cattle of Apollo, reflecting the fact that he's not only the messenger god but also the god of thieves. He is also the *psychopompus* ("sender of souls"), who guides the souls of the dead down to the Underworld. He's a jack-of-all-

---

[40] One of these four, Demeter, will be covered in a later chapter.
[41] These are the only children they have together. No wonder Hera gets so angry when Zeus goes off and has children with other women and goddesses.

trades, in other words, by no means an Alpha like Zeus, Apollo, or Poseidon yet his heraldic function is indispensable to the proper functioning of the Olympian machinery.

We're going to devote the next chapter to Apollo. Artemis (Roman: Diana), his sister, is the goddess of hunting and her epithet *potnia therôn* ("mistress of animals") underscores this fact. As with Apollo, her most conspicuous attribute is her bow and arrow:

Like Athena and Hestia, Artemis is a virgin goddess and as such is not someone to try to seduce or even walk in on unintentionally as she's bathing in the woods, as was the case with the unfortunate hunter Actaeon, whom she turned into a deer, the very prey he was hunting, so his dogs could kill and eat him:

Artemis, more than any other virgin goddess, envies those who have children, both deities (in the case of Aphrodite) and especially mortals. The most famous example of this is Niobe, a mortal woman who has twelve children and brags to Artemis' mother Leto that she has ten more than she does. Not a smart thing to say to a goddess whose son and daughter always wield a bow and arrow. Apollo shoots the six sons, Artemis shoots the six daughters, and none of the arrows miss their mark.

CHAPTER SIX

APOLLO

Apollo missed out on the lottery that took place after the Titanomachy resulting in Zeus, Poseidon, and Hades being lords of the sky, sea, and Underworld, respectively. Not out of any unsuitability on his part to rule over any of these domains (although no one would have wanted Hades' job), but simply because he hadn't been born yet. And that's important: there's some serious competition between Zeus and Apollo that needs to be addressed. They vie for being considered the greatest of the Olympians. So although Apollo considers himself to be worthy of being deemed the number one Olympian, he can't be because Zeus already *is*. That's a significant, potentially insurmountable problem for him: he's just not going to be considered the greatest of the Olympians no matter how hard he tries unless he comes up with a plan. And he does. What is this plan and how does he execute it?

There is a heroic counterpart to Apollo's predicament: when the Greeks go to Troy to fight the Trojan War, Agamemnon is the *nominal* leader of the Greeks because he happens to be the brother of the Spartan king Menelaus, the kidnapping of whose wife Helen is the impetus for the war in the first place. Achilles, however, is by far the greatest of the Greek warriors, many times better than anyone else and everyone acknowledges it, even Agamemnon (however tardily and begrudgingly). This situation is analogous to that between Zeus and Apollo: Zeus is the king of the gods and Apollo accepts that fact but by the same token thinks of himself as intrinsically better even than Zeus (despite Zeus being *physically* stronger; there are undertones here of the Achilles/Odysseus contrast). Whereas Achilles' way of dealing with his unjust subordination to Agamemnon, however, will be to imperil the rest of the Greeks until finally transcending his anger, Apollo finds a more creative outlet for dealing with his problem.

Apollo is not only born *after* Zeus, we need to remember, but also born *of* Zeus. Zeus, as we already know, is the go-to god for impregnating others than his wife, and this time he does it with the goddess we met at the end of last chapter, Leto (Roman: Latona), whom he falls for and seduces and they have not just one kid but two, the twins Apollo and Artemis. Hera, understandably resenting Zeus for having offspring with yet another mate, forces Leto to travel the world to seek a place to give birth to the children who are causing her the same sort of pre-natal pain as Gaea had experienced with the Titans. Finally the inhabitants of a floating island called Delos welcome Leto with open arms. Delos is situated halfway between the east coast of Greece and the west coast of Asia Minor, smack dab in the middle of west and east, symbolic of the fact that Apollo's worship will extend to both parts of the world.[42] As Apollo grows up he too is tutored by the centaur Chiron:

Two Olympian goddesses, Athena and Artemis, come as close as the ancient Greeks allow to the quality of refinement monotheistic religions of the future will attribute to their Supreme Being. Apollo is as close as you get to a *male* version of a somewhat more perfect god than the others, unlike someone else we know. Zeus is the god of justice but that doesn't translate into him being anything resembling a god of perfection. Rather, he's a god of pleasure, constantly seeking out new mates and getting them pregnant, entrusted, like Agamemnon, with a power over others that doesn't necessarily equate to intrinsic superiority. Whereas Zeus is the god of justice and Athena is the goddess of wisdom, Apollo is the god of truth, of *absolute* truth, the kind of truth Socrates would be willing to die for.[43]

---

[42] In the Trojan War, for example, he and Artemis will take the side of the Trojans rather than the Greeks.

[43] And yet he gets a bad rap sometimes as the god of the brain to Dionysus' god of the heart. But is this fair? The reputation Apollo has gotten throughout the ages for being the god of reason *as opposed to* the god of emotion is to some extent a self-fulfilling prophesy, born of an all-too-literalistic reading of Nietzsche's *The Birth of Tragedy*.

Apollo is also the god of lyric poetry, particularly of love songs, reflecting the fact that, while he shares with Zeus a penchant for promiscuity,[44] he becomes more emotionally involved with some of his most famous conquests than Zeus does. Case in point: he falls in love with a girl named Daphne, and although he chooses a hardly endearing way to pursue her (literally, by chasing her through the woods), he is so distraught by not winning her over that when she's transformed into a laurel tree by her solicitous river-god father, from that point on he worships the laurel tree (*daphne*) because he's in love with her and he never loses this love for her:[45]

Apollo is the patron god of Delphi the way Zeus is the patron god of Olympia and Athena is the patron goddess of Athens. The reason Apollo chooses Delphi as the location of his shrine is that it's considered to be the *omphalos* ("belly-button") of the universe. This goes back to the Cronus story, how Rhea takes her parents' advice and substitutes a stone for Zeus so that when Cronus swallows it he vomits it up. Just as Uranus' castrated genitals resulted in the birth of Aphrodite, so Cronus' rejected stone results in something game-changing as well: it flies far away and lands at the foot of a mountain called Parnassus, in a settlement called Delphi, which because of this event is from now on considered to be the *omphalos* of the universe.

---

[44] I'm aware that Apollo's philandering seems to contradict the comment I made above about the relative aura of perfection surrounding him. I submit, however, that within a mythic context the two are not mutually exclusive. Apollo is the teflon god.

[45] The mythic preeminence of the laurel tree is extended to the real world as well in the form of the laurel branch being given as an award to winners of athletic and poetic contests at the Pythian Games at Delphi, one of the four shrines (including Olympia) where Panhellenic games were held (see page 24).

What better place, then, for the shrine of a god who seeks to establish himself as the new Zeus? His intermediary is the Pythia, a priestess named after Python, the giant snaky creature Apollo had to slay to consecrate Delphi:[46]

The Pythia is positioned on a tripod over a cleft in the floor of the temple of Apollo which, although like its Olympian counterpart lies in ruins, one feels a sense of awe when experiencing in its natural setting within the magnificent shrine to Apollo:

---

[46] A feat no less impressive than (and a deliberate *comparandum* with) Zeus, in his final dynastic challenge, slaying the equally formidable Typhon. Yet another example of the man-over-beast theme but also—and more saliently in this context—of the competition between Zeus and Apollo that remains a leitmotif of this book until its final sentence.

The Pythia goes into an ecstatic trance (think "300") from psychotropic fumes emitted from the floor of the temple, which inspire her to channel the truth of Apollo. Although she receives his message directly, however, she conveys it in a cryptic manner, with much room for interpretation, ambiguously enough for the powers-that-be who eventually have it reported to them to interpret any way they wish to, enabling a more sustainable form of propaganda than ever before.

People travel long distances to worship Apollo but he wants to go a step further and provide them with some practical benefit for their trouble. Zeus has the Olympics: what added-value can Apollo bring to the table? He too will oversee athletic contests—the Pythian Games, commemorating his victory over Python—but he takes Delphi to the next level, by establishing it as the *omphalos* of Greece not only in myth but also in reality, where, more than any other place in the world, the course of history is determined. For the kinds of questions asked of the oracle, after the long journey required to reach it, tend to be of the monumental "Do we go to war or not?" variety. In his cosmic competition with Zeus, then, Apollo fares quite well, despite his late head-start. Olympia is where the Olympics take place, Delphi is where war and peace are decided. In the end, Apollo, at the brink of history, establishes himself as the patron god of the *omphalos* of the universe, the god of prophesy at the shrine that will become as crucial to the real world of the future as Olympus was to the mythical world of the past.

CHAPTER SEVEN

DEMETER, DIONYSUS

Demeter (Roman: Ceres) is goddess of the grain, the harvest, agriculture, food. Her Roman name is easy to remember because the word "cereal" comes from it. As to what there is to say about her, that's not why we're devoting more than half a chapter to her. There's not nearly as much to say about her as there is about Zeus or Apollo, because of how central they are to ancient Greek culture. That doesn't mean, however, that Demeter isn't important: she is, but differently than Zeus and Apollo are. Demeter is important the way the next Olympian we're going to talk about, Dionysus, is important: not as a mainstream deity but as an underground deity, founder of a mystery religion, situated (in her case) in a town called Eleusis, thirteen miles north of Athens, a religion whose backstory we're going to consider in this chapter rather than go very far into what we know of the religion itself, which, by definition, isn't much.

In the post-Titanomachy lottery determining which gods are assigned which portions of the universe, Zeus and Poseidon are allotted the sky and sea, respectively, while Hades (Roman: Pluto) is allotted the Underworld. All his siblings are having a blast 24/7 in the most joyful place in existence and he's sitting alone in the place that everyone avoids until they no longer can. Zeus soon realizes, however, that although Hades has been sent to the Underworld fair and square, he and the rest of the Olympians can't be too harsh with him: he eventually has to end up marrying *someone* down there. Who will that someone be?

The story begins like so many others in Greek myth, with Zeus having a child with someone other than Hera. This time it's Demeter. She and Zeus have a child named Persephone. And it's this girl, his own daughter, that Zeus, without so much as consulting with Demeter, is going to serve up to Hades. One day she's picking flowers in a meadow. You already know things aren't going to go well. It's the beginning of a horror movie. The author of the *Homeric Hymn to Demeter* knows you

41

know this and wants to increase the dramatic tension rather than resolve it prematurely, so he dwells for awhile on the flowers that Persephone is picking, points out the ominous fact that they are narcissus flowers and goes into their backstory.

A girl named Echo is frolicking in nature (an echo of where we last saw Persephone) and sees a boy in the distance. As she gets closer to him she notices how good-looking he is. When she gets within earshot of him she finds out that his name is Narcissus. She puts on the charm and tries to seduce him. He ignores her. As a devotee of Artemis he is indifferent to what Aphrodite has to offer. Echo, then, who is herself quite attractive and not used to rejection, settles for sitting down and watching Narcissus do his thing, day after day, for months and years until her body starts fusing with the rocks and all that remains of her is her voice.

She can only speak when spoken to, reflect back to the speaker the final part of what he has just said without him knowing it's not merely a reflection of his own voice but also her speaking to him. By this point the gods have had enough of this guy already: they punish him for not rewarding his stalker with the attention she thinks she deserves. One day he's sitting by a pool of water and he looks down onto its glassy surface. He sees a reflection of his face on it that he becomes so obsessed with that he falls into the water and drowns:

Persephone, then, is picking Narcissus flowers in a meadow (with red in the middle, symbolizing blood) and Zeus offers up his and Demeter's child to Hades: "Okay, go ahead, there she is picking flowers in the meadow, you can go get her, she's your wife." Rather than be decent about it, rather than court Persephone legitimately, rather than take her to the movies, Hades gets into his chariot and rides up from the Underworld through a cleft in the earth and swoops her up into his chariot:

He forces her to go with him to the Underworld, and just as they're entering its gates, Persephone emits such a loud scream that Demeter can hear it at the other end of the world. She searches for her daughter for nine days but in vain.

Helios (who is everywhere all the time, the Forest Gump of Greek myth) eventually informs Demeter of what has happened, including Zeus' role in the incident, but she resumes her search until she reaches Eleusis. She disguises herself as an old woman, enters the town, meets king Celeus, and gets a job as the royal nanny to watch his son and two daughters.

Everything is fine until one night queen Metaneira catches Demeter dipping her son into a fire, not to hurt him but to make him immortal. The queen, however, has no way of knowing this: all she sees is some crazy woman trying to hurt her kid. The queen orders Demeter to stop and because of this affront to her honor (and/or ego), Demeter punishes Metaneira by revealing her divinity and insisting that in the future she and her husband worship her, the patron goddess of Eleusis, and have the people of Eleusis build a temple for her, the Telesterion ("Finishing Room"), where, as far as we know (which we don't), the afterlife was simulated as compellingly as current special-effects technology allowed:

Demeter refuses to give up on her daughter. She becomes so sad, however, misses her daughter so much, that the earth starts dying. Zeus, of course, doesn't want things to stay that way,[47] so he sends the guy you would expect him to send, Hermes, down to the Underworld to try to get Persephone back. Hades agrees to Zeus' request but plays a trick on Persephone: just as she's about to leave the Underworld, Hades gets her to eat four pomegranate seeds, a pledge, unbeknownst to her, of the indissolubility of their marriage. Because of that Persephone has to return to Hades four months a year and continues to do so up to this day, as is evident from the fact that we still have to endure the season of winter.

Dionysus is another god born to Zeus with someone other than Hera, in this case a mortal woman named Semele. Zeus and Semele conceive a child and Hera, predictably, is jealous. It's like a reality show: each episode Zeus has another lover and Hera comes up with another scheme to punish him indirectly by punishing his offspring directly. This time she uses her knowledge that Semele is only in it for the fame of being with the most powerful deity in the universe to her disadvantage: she convinces Semele that the one she thinks is Zeus isn't really Zeus at all but an ordinary mortal pretending to be Zeus. Semele is devastated. As a proto-groupie (appropriate for the mother of Dionysus; think Penny Lane in "Almost Famous") she's only into Zeus for his power, so she needs to find out for sure that it's Zeus she's been courting, otherwise she would consider it to be a waste of time. Zeus, like a Hollywood producer fingering his golden chain, assures Semele, "No, I really *am* the guy you think I am and to prove it I'm going to grant you any wish."

What better request could Semele make than to ask him to prove he's in fact king of the gods by revealing himself to her in all his glory, the way the other gods see him? This is not something to ask of Zeus, however, because the only way a mortal can safely look at him is if he wears a disguise to temper his otherwise overwhelming power. Her request, then, results in her own destruction (careful what you wish for):

---

[47] The same way the CEO of a corporation doesn't want its workers to go on strike.

Remember, though, that Semele is pregnant when this happens. What about the child? Just before Semele is cremated on a funeral pyre, Zeus removes the fetus from her womb and inserts it into his own thigh until the god of wine is ready to be born:

Grapes, like olives, are staples of ancient Greece, one of the few things that can grow well there. Along with grapes come wine and along with wine comes inebriation and the altered state of mind it entails. Appropriately, various part-animal, part-human creatures with wild natures are associated with Dionysus, as a metaphor for drunkenness as well as, paradoxically, the kind of beast-like qualities that other, less earthy gods and heroes tend to single out for man-vs.-beast scapegoating:

Like Demeter, Dionysus is an earth god, despite being an Olympian. He lives officially in Olympus (that's where his PO box is) but he wanders all over the earth because he loves people and wants to be with them. The devotees of Dionysus consider themselves to be inspired by him, enthused by him (Greek *enthousiasmos* and Latin *inspiratio* both signify a divine "breathing into" humans). Maenads ("crazy women"), the primary followers of Dionysus, claim that doing so results in psychotropic bliss, a surrender to ecstasy. The ancient Greek word *ecstasis* means "to stand outside of." Outside of what? What one normally stands inside of: a life of quotidian drudgery. Yes, the ancient Greeks had their version of that too. Especially women, slaves, and others prevented from taking part in the *demos* part of "democracy." They acknowledged these kinds of emotions—and the mystery religions that provided a platform for them—to be necessary and advantageous to living a full life, which is why there was a god devoted to wine who, paradoxically, was taken very seriously.

A tragedy by Euripides (480-406 BC) called the *Bacchae* provides us with indispensable insight into the importance of Dionysus to the ancient Greeks and to women in particular. Its main theme is the disastrous repercussions that ensue when people are prevented by those in power from worshipping the wine god, from confronting and embracing the deepest aspects of themselves and each other. The play opens with Dionysus on a PR campaign all over Greece. He's heartened by the fact that people are generally being allowed to worship him. In Thebes, however, he's having some trouble: some are even denying he's a god.[48] Even his aunt Agave denies his divinity, a situation he rectifies by possessing her with the overwhelming desire to become a maenad. The king of Thebes, Agave's son Pentheus, however, has a special dislike for this proto-Elvis and the dissident energy he exudes.

Once Dionysus discovers that the reason so many Thebans have been neglecting his altars is that Pentheus has been perjuring him,

---

[48] Keep in mind that he already has a chip on his shoulder at the outset because of his half-mortal origins. It's not a Zeus-like situation where he's unequivocally divine; rather, he's someone who constantly feels he has to fight for his respect.

claiming he's not even partially divine, he possesses Pentheus too, not to become one of his followers, however, but to be curious enough about what the maenads are doing in the woods (with definite sexual undertones) to induce him to disguise himself as a woman and spy on them from a tree. He gets away with it for awhile but the maenads eventually see him and climb the tree and throw him down from it and pounce on him while in a frenzy and begin ripping him apart. One of the women ripping him apart, in a stroke of tragic irony, is none other than Agave, who discovers too late what she has been doing to her son.

CHAPTER EIGHT

HADES

It is instructive to compare the Heaven/Hell division of the universe common to monotheistic religions with the way the Greeks saw things. The idea of Olympus begins with a particular mountain in northern Greece but becomes more abstract over time, takes on the otherwordly properties we associate with the concept of Heaven. If pressed to say where Olympus was located, an ancient Greek could point to the mountain and leave it at that. It's such a tall mountain, however, that clouds often skirt the top of it, leaving to the imagination what's above them, imbuing Olympus with an aura of mystery. Above all, though, there is a major difference between Olympus and Heaven: whereas righteous people are supposed to end up in Heaven, Olympus is where the twelve Olympians live but never humans.

Analogously, an ancient Greek temple, terrestrial counterpart to Olympus, is not intended for people to conglomerate in but to house the statue of the patron god or goddess the *polis* in question worships. Hell is where the opposite of people who go to Heaven go. For the ancient Greeks, the Underworld is where *everybody* goes after they die as long as they've been properly buried. If they haven't been properly buried they become ghosts and their spirits flit around for eternity. The Underworld, then, doesn't have the bad connotations of Hell *per se*, although it's bad in the sense that anyone would rather live as long as they could on earth than go down to it, no matter how much power they might exert over their fellow inmates.

The best example of this is when Odysseus visits Achilles in the Underworld and tells him how lucky he is to be the king of everyone down there: "Achilleus, no man before has been more blessed than you, nor ever will be. Before, when you were still alive, we Argives honored you as we did the gods, and now in this place you have great authority over the dead. Do not grieve, even in death, Achilleus." Achilles says:

"O shining Odysseus,[49] never try to console me for dying. I would rather follow the plow as thrall to another man, one with no land allotted him and not much to live on, than be a king over all the perished dead."

The notion of life as a means to an end, a rehearsal to perfect oneself in order to deserve an afterlife of eternal bliss, was alien to the early Greeks, something they didn't believe in until late in their history in the form of the Elysian Fields, the opposite of Tartarus, where some of the greatest heroes went to live forever. In general, however, the Greeks believed that life on earth was all there was: enjoy it while you can, *carpe diem*, for when it's all over and your soul goes down to the Underworld, it sucks, period.[50]

"Hades" means "the invisible one," reflecting the fact that no one knows what he looks like and very little art depicts him. His Roman name Pluto ("Wealthy One") is blatantly ironic, since he's bestowing on people the ultimate in impoverishment, replacing a life on earth with a lack of life in the Underworld. He is also called *polydegmon*, "receiver of many," and *polyxenos*, "host of many," because he has many guests there, which is also ironic, this idea that he's a host to many: a host, yes, but the worst kind of host there is, the host of those who would rather be anywhere but where he's hosting them.

Odysseus goes down to the Underworld to consult with the blind seer Tiresias, who has key information about how to get home (recalling Perseus and the Graeae).[51] Before finding Tiresias, however, he encounters others such as Elpinor, a minor character from the Homeric oeuvre, a shade who flits around aimlessly because he isn't able to get any kind of repose until he's buried properly on earth:

---

[49] The Greek reads *polymechanos*, more accurately translated "much-devising," which is a common Homeric epithet for Odysseus (used twenty-three times in the Homeric corpus), but here it's being used ironically because Odysseus is supposed to be the most intelligent of all the Greeks yet he is proving to be clueless with respect to what Achilles is about to tell him.

[50] There are loopholes, however, such as apotheosis: the deification of a mortal, the idea that although there's no Heaven you at least have the possibility that if you're a good enough hero you might be so blessed that you become a god, like Heracles. Or Caesar.

[51] See footnote 18.

Odysseus eventually finds Tiresias and, behind him, his mother Anticlea, who, it turns out, has killed herself out of despair for Odysseus' absence from Ithaca, believing he was dead and that she might be able to visit him in the Underworld. Odysseus, telling his hosts, the Phaeacians, this story later on, will say: "My tears welled up when I saw her and pity filled all my heart, but grieved though I was I dared not let her approach me until I should learn the future from Tiresias.":

This epitomizes Odysseus' refusal (or at least an intention to refuse[52]) to neglect his original purpose for going to the Underworld: to find out what he has to do to get home. He misses his wife and needs to establish harmony in his household, which for the Ithacans is more than just a place to live because he's their king and the state of his palace represents either the chaos or the order of the kingdom as a whole.

Before leaving the Underworld, Odysseus visits Tartarus, where he encounters various characters linked by different types of hubristic behavior. Tityus is there for trying to rape Leto, mother of Apollo and Artemis (which you don't go doing), and his punishment is similar to that of Prometheus (whom we'll get to): he has his liver eaten by birds (in this case vultures), as a symbol of the curtailment of sexual desire, which the liver was believed to be the seat of:

---

[52] Unsuccessfully at first but then, after sowing his wild oats and getting his priorities straight, ultimately successfully.

Tantalus' crime was to test out whether the culinary preparation of his son Pelops (of chariot-race fame) would be detected by the gods (think the end of "The Cook, the Thief, His Wife, and Her Lover"). Everyone saw through it but Demeter. His punishment is to be "tantalized" for eternity, to live in a pool of water over which fruit is hanging, but when he raises his head to get closer to it, it rises just a little out of reach, and when he lowers his head to drink some water, it recedes, resulting in permanent hunger and thirst:

Another notorious inhabitant of Tartarus, with a complicated backstory that also has to do with challenging the authority of the gods, is Sisyphus, who for the rest of eternity has to roll a giant boulder up a hill and as soon as he gets to the top of it, just before the boulder is able to be pushed over the edge of the hill and his torment to be thereby concluded, it rolls back toward him all the way down to the foot of the hill, and he has to repeat the process over and over again for eternity:

We end our tour of the Underworld with the myth of Orpheus, son of Calliope (Muse of epic poetry), grandson of Zeus, the most famous musician in the world. His music is so enchanting that it casts a spell not only on gods and humans (and in particular women, who throng about him like Beliebers) but on animals as well:

One day, Eurydice, Orpheus' wife, is being chased around by a man named Aristaeus, son of Apollo (like father like son), and she's bitten by a snake and killed. Orpheus is determined to get her out of the Underworld, convinced it isn't fair for her to be there yet (think "Heaven Can Wait"). So he, Odysseus-like, takes a trip to the Underworld, and once he gets there it's obvious he doesn't belong there: he sneaks in and is confronted by its permanent inhabitants and told he needs to get out but he plays his music and suddenly his listeners are transfixed:

Hades, no less under the spell of Orpheus' music than anyone else, agrees to release Euridice on condition that Orpheus not look back before leaving. At the last minute, however, he is so distrustful of Hades' word (who wouldn't be?), and longs so much for Euridice, that he looks behind him and at that moment she disappears forever:

CHAPTER NINE

PERSEUS

Up to now we have focused almost exclusively on gods and goddesses. In the next four chapters we're going to deal with four heroes, the most important ones before the Trojan War, when others will take their place, grounded more in legend than pure myth, a step closer to history but with a foot still in the fictional realm. For the Greeks and Romans these worlds overlapped to an alarming degree, culminating in Augustus, the first Roman Emperor (protégé of Caesar, Alexander, and Achilles, themselves masters of myth) employing myth-making techniques to legitimate his reign and prevent himself from suffering the fate of his adoptive father (and posthumous god[53]) Julius Caesar.

Tradition has it that Perseus started it all, first in a long line of Greek heroes. Probably not. What he *is*, though, is the first Greek hero we *know* of, the best publicized one. How did he get that way? What did he do to assure he would still be talked about by later generations? It wasn't enough to be great: plenty of others were. He had to distinguish himself by transcending his human condition, by *mythologizing* himself. Like Gilgamesh, he knew he couldn't do it by becoming more divine: he would never be more than partially a god, and that was not good enough. So he did the next best thing: he invented product placement.

The story of Perseus begins with Acrisius, king of Argos,[54] who has a problem that applies only to heroes, not to gods. The problem of Uranus, Cronus, and Zeus was how to avoid being overthrown by their children. Otherwise they never worried about who would rule next because they would never die. This is not true for heroes. Mortals, even kings, have to die, and thus they *do* need to worry about succession. If they don't, their subjects will begin to worry about having someone cruel

---

[53] The Romans too were fond of paradox.
[54] One of the oldest Mycenaean settlements whose kings would eventually go to the Trojan War. Notice that all of the heroes we'll be featuring in the next four chapters perform their most important exploits *before* the Trojan War, the backdrop of the *Iliad*.

thrust upon them once their current king dies. So a king, in both the mythic and real worlds, has to make clear who his successor is.

Acrisius doesn't know, because he doesn't have a son to stand next in line as the king of Argos. This matters more and more the older he becomes until he does what anyone does who has a sufficiently consequential question to ask: he travels to the oracle at Delphi. As as is often the case with oracles, he finds out the answer to a question he didn't ask: his *daughter* will have a son who is destined to kill him. But what can he do? Does he do what Uranus did and prevent the children from being born? Does he do what Cronus did and deal with them *after* they've been born? No, he goes a step further: he prevents his daughter, Danaë, from having sex at all, from even making contact with men by locking her away in a tower. There's a portal in the ceiling of the tower, however, that Zeus (who else?) sees her through and he falls in lust with her (of course) and, as a shower of gold, enters the tower with her and mates with her, thereby conceiving Perseus, first of the Greek heroes:

Time goes on and Danaë hides her baby bump from Acrisius. When she gives birth she tries to hide that fact too until one day the baby cries so loudly that Acrisius discovers what's going on and locks them both up in a chest (recalling Osiris and Seth) and tosses them into the sea:

 Danaë and Perseus eventually wash up on the island of Seriphos. Someone opens up the chest, a fisherman named Dictys, an ordinary man except for the fact that his brother is the king. King Polydectes[55] falls in lust with Danaë but Perseus is getting old enough to be a nuisance to him, a potential obstacle to winning over his mother. So the king feigns engagement to a different woman, Hippodameia, and orders everyone but Perseus—who doesn't get the memo—not to bother showing up to the wedding unless they also bring a gift for him.

On the wedding day, everyone comes with a gift but, of course, Perseus. Polydectes unjustly chastises him, who, falling into Polydectes' trap, offers to compensate for his putative oversight by giving Polydectes any gift he might wish for (recalling Semele), even the head of the infamous Gorgon Medusa. "Okay," laughs Polydectes, "go kill the Gorgon Medusa," a challenge no one has ever yet been able to meet. Perseus agrees and prepares to go on his hero-quest, the first one in Greek mythstory.

The thing about Gorgons, besides having snaky hair and being scary-looking, is that if you look at them you turn to stone. Perseus, then, is going to have to be especially careful. This is going to be a story of ingenuity, as will also be the case with his great-grandson Heracles, who will embark on an equally (or even more) famous journey, conquering one obstacle after another until he finally achieves his ultimate goal. Perseus' hero-quest, however, involves a single goal rather than twelve, as will be the case for Odysseus, who is thus in this sense perhaps a better analogue for Perseus.

---

[55] The "dectes" part of his name shares the same root as Dictys; *poly* means "many," so his name implies that he's the greater of the two brothers, which begs the question: will the events of the story bear out this etymology? If not, his name is ironic.

It remains to be seen how Perseus (spoiler alert) manages to pull off this unprecedented feat. There are three stages to the story.[56] The first consists of Perseus consulting with the Graeae, sisters of the Gorgons, who share a single eye and a single tooth between them by passing them around when they need them. Perseus has to time the transfer of the eye from one woman to another so he can grab it and bribe them by insisting that unless they tell him what he needs to know, they won't get their eye back. What he needs to know is where he can locate certain nymphs, the Hesperides, who will provide him with the equipment he needs to accomplish his goal.

The Graeae eventually tell Perseus where to find the nymphs, who, in the second stage of the story, provide him with a sword, Hades' cap of invisibility, Hermes' winged sandals, and the *kibisis*, a bag Perseus is going to have to put Medusa's head into without looking at it first.[57] The third and final stage of Perseus' quest consists of locating Medusa and, with an ingenuity foreshadowing that of the other heroes we'll be dealing with, using his shield as a rear-view mirror to help him locate her and kill her, thus completing his quest:

[56] As with the Succession Myth of Uranus, Cronus, and Zeus. It's doubtful this structural correspondence between the first divine myth and the first heroic myth is coincidental.
[57] This collaborative effort by various gods to help out Perseus foreshadows its heroic counterpart in the journey of the Argonauts we'll be getting to in the JASON chapter.

Perseus puts Medusa's head into the *kibisis* and flies away via Hermes' winged sandals. On his way back to Seriphos he happens to fly over a maiden in distress as she's about to be sacrificed to a sea monster to appease the wrath of Poseidon, who is sticking up for his friends the Nereids, sea creatures who got wind of the fact that Cassiopea, queen of Ethiopia,[58] boasted she was more beautiful than they were. The only way the king and queen can save their kingdom is to sacrifice their daughter to the sea monster.[59]

Perseus swoops down, slays the sea monster (another variation of the man-against-beast theme, with echoes of Medusa, further establishing Perseus as the original beast-slayer), and carries Andromeda away:

When they arrive in Seriphos, Perseus prepares to deliver Medusa's head to Polydectes. He finds out, however, that the king has been behaving badly towards his mother. He warns Danaë to look away, removes

---

[58] Foreign, exotic locales are a frequent ingredient of hero-quests in a world where a lack of quick and easy transportation requires a kind of heroism even to be able to visit such places, let alone to perform superhuman feats in them.

[59] This anticipates Agamemnon, nominal king of the Greek fleet, sacrificing his daughter Iphigenia to procure favorable winds to sail to Troy to fight the Trojan War. This act, predictably, riles his wife Clytemnestra enough for her to retaliate against him to his marked disadvantage, as we'll see in the AFTER TROY chapter.

Medusa's head from the *kibisis*, and turns Polydectes to stone. From then on Dictys the fisherman rules benignly as king of Seriphos. Perseus and Andromeda get married and have Electryon, who has Alcmene, who, with Zeus, has Heracles, greatest hero of the Greeks, great grandson of Perseus, first hero of the Greeks.

We still haven't answered the question, though, of how Perseus manages to get himself remembered forever as the first Greek hero. By now Athena is quite impressed by him, especially for how resourcefully he used her shield, the famous *aegis* given to her by Zeus. How can he parlay her affection for him into a PR campaign? He points out to her that now that Medusa is dead, they don't have to settle for a reflection of her head on the shield anymore: now they can place the real thing onto it, to commemorate Perseus' unprecedented achievement as well as to capitalize on the apotropaic ("scaring away") properties of the shield itself, which benefits Athena. In other words, it's a win-win proposition. Athena is overjoyed by the idea and Perseus gives her Medusa's severed head to attach to her shield, so that whenever anyone sees it they'll automatically think of Perseus, due to his having, in effect, reserved advertising space on it:

CHAPTER TEN

HERACLES

Perseus and Andromeda have two children, a boy named Alcaeus and a girl named Electryon. Alcaeus gets married and has a boy named Amphytrion. Electryon gets married and has a girl named Alcmena. The cousins Amphytrion and Alcmena get married. One day, Amphytrion is away from home and Zeus (who else?) falls in lust with Alcmena and (what else?) has sex with her. Later that day, Amphytrion returns home and also has sex with her. Twins are born, Iphicles, son of Amphytrion, and Heracles (Roman: Hercules), son of Zeus. Notice that because of the Perseus connection on his mother's side, Heracles is more than a demigod (literally "half" a god). In the next chapter we're going to encounter a hero who possesses in some accounts less than half the divinity of Heracles, in other accounts more than less than half. And yet they are both often referred to as "demigods." What's going on here?

The Greeks didn't make a big deal out of how much divinity their heroes had. The most salient fact is not how much divinity a hero has, nor even *that* he is partially divine, but rather that he *isn't fully* divine and that he therefore has to die. This should remind you of Gilgamesh who, despite being three-quarters divine, was still mortal. So are Perseus and Heracles, and all other heroes. That's what makes them heroes rather than gods. And because they're heroes and have to die, they're potential tragic figures whose suffering will mean more to us mortals who tell their stories than the occasional inconveniences of the gods. That's why mortals rather than immortals are the protagonists of epics and tragedies.

The story of Heracles is just as much Hera's story as it is his own. It's the most famous iteration of Hera's frequent preoccupation with punishing not Zeus but his offspring born to someone other than herself. When the Titan Prometheus tries to trick Zeus about a certain sacrifice we'll get into in the JASON chapter, Zeus *knows* what he is up to and lets him get away with it to store up ammunition to punish him in the future. In this story, on the other hand, Zeus actually gets fooled, by none other than Hera.[60] Before Heracles is born, an oracle proclaims that the next child born in the universe will end up being the next king of Mycenae. Zeus is excited about the news, aware that Alcmena is about to give birth to their child. Hera, who will do all she can to prevent him from being born next, expedites the birth of Heracles' cousin Eurystheus, another descendant of Perseus, so that he rather than Heracles will be the prophesized king. Zeus can't believe how badly he's been duped, but that's the least of it. Hera is not satisfied merely with Heracles not being king. From now on she will do all she can to make life miserable for this son of Zeus ironically, cruelly (from Hera's standpoint), and hilariously (from our standpoint)[61] named "Glory of Hera."

Hera's first attempt to sabotage Heracles occurs when he is still an infant: she puts snakes into his crib so they will kill him. He kills them instead:

This is no fluke: as Heracles grows up it becomes clear he's not someone to mess with. As a boy, for example, his music teacher Linus tells him he's terrible at playing music. So he kills him, exhibiting the short fuse he will become infamous for and adumbrating his ultimate crime:

---

[60] She will fool him again in the *Iliad* when she distracts him from the battlefield so the Greeks can regain the advantage they had over the Trojans before Achilles bowed out of the fighting. Although Hera is often disrespected by Zeus, she is no more a pushover than Hephaestus.

[61] It's worth mentioning that the element of humor plays a larger part in stories about Heracles than about any other hero, despite (or perhaps because of, as a form of comic relief for) the tragedy otherwise surrounding him.

Heracles marries Megara, princess of Thebes (where Heracles is from), and they have three children. Hera's next attempt to sabotage Heracles is unfortunately more successful. Recognizing the futility of sending others to kill him, she goes directly to the source: she drives him insane enough to induce him to perform an act he would never think of performing were he in his right mind: he slaughters his own children:

Whereas Polydectes had arranged for Perseus *not* to do something (i.e., bring a gift to his wedding) to induce him to compensate for it by attempting to kill Medusa (the implication being that it would end up killing him instead), Hera arranges for Heracles to *do* something (i.e., kill his children) to induce him to compensate for it in a way she hopes will imperil him. Heracles goes to Delphi and asks what he needs to do to atone for what he takes responsibility for doing despite not having been in his right mind while doing it. The Pythia (in cahoots with Hera)[62] instructs him to go to Mycenae and atone for killing his children by performing the Twelve Labors that will be assigned to him by none other than Eurystheus himself, king of Mycenae instead of Heracles because of the switcheroo pulled by Hera at their birth.

The first of Heracles' labors is to kill the Nemean Lion, which has been terrorizing the countryside for years because no one has been able to kill it. Heracles does so, not by the use of weapons, which the lion is immune to, but by strangling it with his bare hands, thereby displaying his supreme strength:

After killing the lion, Heracles skins it and wears its head and hide as his costume from now on, no less inseparable from him than the beard of Zeus or Poseidon:

This will have resonance in the real world as well for Alexander the Great, who will portray himself on coins as the second-coming of Heracles (or maybe Heracles himself: the fact that we don't know for sure is precisely the point):

---

[62] Delphigate

The Roman emperor Commodus (the bad guy in the movie "Gladiator") went even further by coopting Heracles' club as well, his counterpart to Zeus' thunderbolt and Poseidon's trident:

Heracles' next labor is his first display of ingenuity: to kill the Lernean Hydra, his counterpart to Zeus' Typhon and Apollo's Python but with a twist: rather than a giant monster with the body of a snake, the Hydra is a giant monster with many poisonous snaky arms that multiply whenever they're cut off. Heracles, then, has to come up with a way to dispatch the beast without making the same mistake others have made in the past, resulting in an unwieldy number of arms to deal with. To this end, Heracles cuts off one arm at a time and immediately cauterizes each stump so it can't grow back:

Rather than catalog the next ten labors I prefer to stand back a little and consider the terrain upon which they were performed, the first six anyway,[63] to remark on how their spatial orientation exhibits a similar centralizing tendency as what we saw when we looked at the map of Panhellenic shrines in the ZEUS, HERA chapter (see page 24):

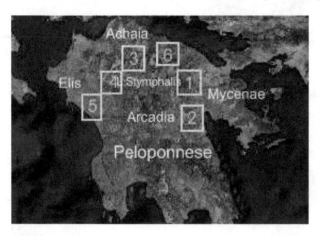

There are obvious differences, of course: the Panhellenic shrines are places Greeks traveled to in the real world, while the sites of the Twelve Labors are places Heracles traveled to in the mythic world. Still, whether you travel to the former physically or the latter imaginarily, a similar principle is at work here, a collective assumption that the various *poleis* around Greece collaborate in a geographical project that transcends local concerns and fosters a sense of everyone belonging to the same Greek community. These kinds of things don't just happen on their own.

---

[63] Nemean Lion, Lernaean Hydra, Ceryneian Hind, Erymanthian Boar, Augean Stables, Stymphalian Birds

CHAPTER ELEVEN

THESEUS

In this chapter we're going to rekindle the distinction we made earlier between what a myth says and how it's used. We dealt with propaganda in connection with Narmer and that's what we're going to be doing again with Theseus. Theseus was used differently, as a hero, by the Greeks than Perseus and Heracles. While the latter two were worshipped all over Greece, Theseus was indigenous to one *polis* only: Athens.[64] And it's through the Theseus myth that Athens is able to establish herself for the first time as the new kid on the block, the way Apollo did at Delphi.

Theseus, like Perseus and Heracles, lived out his legendary career in Greek prehistory. His myth was not nearly as well-known in early Greece, however, as those of Perseus and Heracles, and only really took off in the historical era, when it was appropriated by the Athenians as a way to dramatize Theseus taking away the leadership of Greece from king Minos of Crete, making it clear that while Minos was the leader of formerly dominant Crete, Theseus is now the leader of newly dominant Athens.

Recall Perseus: interesting birth, interesting upbringing, locked up with Danaë by her father who is paranoid about being overtaken like Uranus, Cronus, and Zeus had been, and Perseus establishing his greatness by defeating the Gorgon Medusa. With these heroes there's one image associated with each of them that stands out from the rest. That's where the idea of an icon, avatar, or brand comes from. With Perseus it's Medusa, symbolizing civilization over lack of civilization, reason over darkness. Same thing with Heracles: interesting birth, driven

---

[64] There's a prosaic reason for our focusing on Athens more than on any other *polis*: it's the source of most of our extant literature, history, philosophy, vases, paintings, and sculptures. And yet it was also intrinsically most culturally important as well. Athens, then, constitutes our best shot at arriving at a more or less accurate understanding of an ancient Greek *polis*. We can't do that with Sparta, for example, except to some extent in its early years, through its lyric poetry, when their *polis* was culturally rich enough to compete creatively with its contemporaries. Then it became a police state.

insane by Hera, having to perform the Twelve Labors. His avatar is the Nemean Lion headdress, representing the fact that he is able to overpower a beast that no one else can, just like Perseus did with Medusa. Athens knows that in order to create the kind of myth that will entrench itself in the collective consciousness—*become a meme*, in other words—and inspire its poets to create tragedies that perpetuate it, they must conform to this mold, this pattern of interesting birth, interesting upbringing, iconic ultimate achievement. So what are these things for Theseus?

King Aegeus of Athens finds himself in a predicament different from the ones we've encountered so far. It's not a matter of his finding out he's going to have a child who will overtake him, but rather that he can't have any children period—or rather *male* children, which amounts to the same thing when dynastic issues are concerned. He's starting to feel pressure from his subjects, who wonder who will take his place. He needs to know whether or not he'll have a male heir. So what does he do? He does what Athenians, not coincidentally, will continue to do in the future, when the mythic world of Theseus transmutes into the real world of Pericles: he travels to the oracle at Delphi, where Apollo is positioning himself as the new Zeus, the go-to god for resolving the issues that matter most, the Prime Mover of history. In the same way, Theseus will establish himself, not as the new Heracles (that is impossible), but as the new *Minos*.

The oracle, however, confuses Aegeus: he doesn't know how to interpret it. So he travels to a place close to Athens called Troezen where king Pittheus, a friend of his, lives. He shares with Pittheus what the oracle told him and asks him if he understands it. Pittheus pretends not to but really does: Aegeus must abstain from sex until he returns to Athens so that the next king will be of pure Athenian stock. Pittheus, however, doing his best to assure that the next Athenian king has Troezenian blood in his veins, gets Aegeus drunk one night and has his daughter Aethra seduce him. They have sex. Later that night Poseidon (rather than Zeus, a twist on the Heracles myth) has sex with her too. A child is conceived, with two fathers, one mortal, the other immortal (another twist on the

Heracles myth). It is less important that Theseus come from Poseidon in particular than that he does *not* come from Zeus, because the new champion of Greece must not have the same father, not necessarily as the hero he seeks to emulate (Heracles), but as the hero he seeks to overcome (Minos).[65]

Aegeus prepares to go back to Athens. Before doing so, however, he asks Aethra to raise the boy—who will be named Theseus ("the Institutionalizer")—in Troezen and instruct him, once he's old enough, to take the hundred-mile journey to Athens and help him out against his rivals. "But how will I know he's old enough?" she asks. "I have placed a sword and sandals under this rock," he answers, pointing to it, "once he's old enough to lift up the rock, he'll be old enough to join me in Athens. Otherwise, if he arrives too soon, the rivals will kill him."

Theseus gets old enough, lifts up the rock, and takes out the sword and sandals. We can only imagine his excitement, barely into adulthood, glorying in his superhuman strength, shouting at the top of his lungs, "I'm going to be a hero!" which really means "I get to be like Heracles!" For by now buzz about Heracles is in the air, the hero other heroes want to emulate. So when Aethra tells him to go to Athens and that she has a ship waiting for him, he insists on taking his journey by land, the way real heroes do. And on his journey he, like Heracles, encounters several obstacles, also referred to as "labors." Only, while Heracles underwent *twelve* labors, Theseus undergoes *six*, exactly half as many, symbolizing the fact that while Heracles is his model, the Athenians are only willing to attribute to him half as much greatness as the hero of heroes Heracles. Theseus, in other words, is Mini-Heracles.

---

[65] Understanding this prevents us from having to bother memorizing who Theseus' immortal father is. The facts fall into place when considered in context like this. Who said genealogy was boring?

Another difference between the labors of the two heroes is that while Heracles' labors routinely involve magical creatures, all but one of Theseus' labors involve *human* adversaries, criminals and bullies he defeats to prevent them from tormenting others in the future. Thus, while the Athenians concede that Theseus is a lesser hero than Heracles,[66] his heroism is nonetheless based more on the sorts of everyday challenges Athenians encounter in their own lives than on the rarified challenges of a Perseus or a Heracles. Like Apollo, Theseus acknowledges his official subordination to his mentor yet at the same time carves out for himself a niche that will ingratiate him with history.

Theseus' *modus operandi* is to give the bullies he encounters a taste of their own medicine. Sinis ("Pinebender"), for example, stands by a tree and whenever someone walks by he offers to show it to him. Once the stranger gets close to the tree, Sinis pulls back on it like a slingshot and flings him to his death. So what does Theseus do?[67] He catches Sinis trying to pull the same trick on him and turns the tables, putting Sinis in his own tree, pulling it like a slingshot, and flinging *him* to *his* death:

Heracles' labors were all over the map, lacking a unified theme, representing brute force, ingenuity, resourcefulness, and so on. Theseus' labors, on the other hand, are linked by the common theme of retributive justice, especially with respect to the custom of *xenia* ("guest-friendship"). And why would that be important? Because Theseus is going to end up being a king of Athens and it's important for the Athenians to establish from the outset that he will be of the upright variety.

---

[66] Mainly to appease the disillusionment of other *poleis* with Athenian exceptionalism.

[67] Before we get to that we need to be clear on the cultural ramifications of Sinis' behavior. The ancient Greeks took the idea of hospitality, of treating strangers well, extremely seriously. Sinis' behavior, then, represents the polar opposite of how a civilized person is expected to behave. Theseus, on the other hand, by punishing Sinis, symbolizes the legal rights eventually vindicated in Athenian law courts.

Theseus, then, goes on his hero-quest and performs his six labors, half as many as Heracles, which amounts to Athens saying, "Okay, on the one hand we're going to create our own indigenous hero and celebrate him, worship him, the way we do Heracles, but on the other hand, don't worry, rest of Greece, we're not saying he's as important as Heracles, whom we all worship in common. Heracles is still just as much *our* biggest hero as he is yours, it's just that we now have an *indigenous* hero as well." But why do that? Why adopt a different hero to be the indigenous hero of Athens? That's where the next leg of the myth comes in, when Athens welds the myth of Minos—founder and first king of Crete, land of the Minoans, first prehistoric civilization of ancient Greece—to the myth of Theseus to commemorate the shift of political power from Crete to Athens once myth turns into history.

King Minos is living in bliss on the island of Crete, thanking the gods for how great everything is (always a dangerous thing to do: things can only get worse), and he asks them to show him a sign that it's not just a fluke, that, as it seems to him, he's truly in their favor. Poseidon hears him and answers his prayers by sending a beautiful bull from the sea. Minos is overjoyed, his prayers having been answered. There's only one problem, though: Minos likes the bull a bit too much. He knows Poseidon expects him to sacrifice it but he can't get himself to do it. This introduces an element to the story that on the face of it seems innocent enough (Minos is a good guy) but will ultimately be capitalized on for propagandistic purposes.

Poseidon, no less (perhaps more) concerned than the other Olympians with saving face, can't afford to sit around thinking, "That Minos is such a nice guy not sacrificing that bull that I just sent him." Rather, he has to *punish* Minos for not doing what he knows Minos knows he expects of him. And here's where the story gets weird, more so than any story we've dealt with so far. Sure, Medusa is creepy, but the weirdness we encounter now is based not on character but on plot, on what Poseidon *does* to punish Minos: *he causes his wife Pasiphaë to want to have sex with the bull.*

Problem is, the bull is just not that into Pasiphaë. So she has to

71

figure out some way to induce him to reciprocate her lust. She goes to Daedalus, the human version of Hephaestus, and has him make for her, alas, a hollow cow she can fit into to trick the bull into believing she is herself a cow:

Pasiphaë fits perfectly into the fake cow:

The bull takes notice, and things take their course:

---

[68] Picasso went through a Minotaur phase in the 1930s, best exemplified by his *Guernica*.

It gets worse: they conceive a child. It gets even worse than that: the child is the Minotaur:

He has a bull's head and a human body. He is the new Medusa, the new Nemean Lion, symbol of the wild beast, the opposite of a civilized human being, the *other*. More than that, however: he's also an opportunity for the Athenians to portray Minos in a (more) positive light (than if he were to kill the Minotaur): everyone on the island of Crete is horrified by this monster but instead of killing him Minos lets him live in a giant labyrinth he has Daedalus build for him, which is inspired by the "labyrinthine" quality of his own palace at Knossos:

At some point Minos' son Androgeus gets killed during a freak accident at an athletic contest in Athens.[69] Minos is so angry at the Athenians for the death of his son that he imposes on them the following penalty:[70] an annual shipment of seven boys and seven girls to Crete to be placed inside the labyrinth for the Minotaur to kill and eat. This is the old, less civilized world the Athenians are bringing to a much-anticipated end through a myth in which Theseus leads them into a future where they rather than the Minoans will run the show. Which begs the question: if Minos is so cruel, why did the Athenians portray him in such a positive light earlier? The operative word here is "earlier": this is a story of change, of a once power-worthy king becoming unworthy of the power he once wielded.

---

[69] You see what has just happened? Suddenly Athens has entered the picture. Not a very smooth segue but a segue all the same: Athens is now associated with Crete in the very same myth.

[70] Notice that at this point in the story Crete is so much more powerful than Athens that they're in the position to be able to punish her at all let alone as harshly as the following:

After three years of horrific sacrifices to appease the anger of Minos, Theseus decides to accompany the next group of children to be sent to the slaughter. He enters the labyrinth with them, aided by a ball of string (and, more importantly, the idea for it) provided to him by Ariadne, Minos' daughter, who instructs him to unfurl it as he passes through the labyrinth so he can retrace his steps after killing the Minotaur. He does so, and from that moment on the Minotaur is to Theseus what Medusa is to Perseus and the Nemean Lion is to Heracles:

Theseus will become the new symbol of Athens, not only while he's king but half a millennium later, when he and the Minotaur will be used symbolically to remind people of Athens and Persia as automatically as Athena reminds them of Perseus and Medusa. All this lies far in the future, however. In the meantime we return to Theseus' own times, when he and his mentor Heracles (who now considers him a kind of equal, the way A-listers do with other A-listers) will accompany our final pre-Trojan War hero on a new, even bigger sort of hero-quest.

CHAPTER TWELVE

JASON

Aeson is the king of Iolcus, a Greek *polis* 200 miles northwest of Athens. His brother Pelias overthrows him, usurps his throne, and decides he's going to kill the entire male population of Iolcus to start over again, to get rid of any trace of those who might rebel against him. Jason, Aeson's son, still a little boy, is sneaked away even further north in Thessaly, far from the things transpiring in Iolcus. He, like Perseus, Heracles, and Theseus before him is tutored by the centaur Chiron. Meanwhile, Pelias receives a particularly puzzling message from the oracle at Delphi: "You will be killed by a man with one sandal." He tucks this information away in the back of his mind and resolves to kill any man he might see wearing a single sandal.

Jason eventually gets old enough to return to Iolcus. Just as Theseus didn't go to Athens to help Aegeus until he could lift the rock with the sword and sandals under it, so Jason must become a man before he can return to Iolcus to usurp the throne from Pelias, who stole it from his father. On the way to Iolcus, Jason helps an elderly woman cross a river, who turns out to be Hera. From this point on he becomes one of her favorites. While helping Hera cross the river, however, Jason loses one of his sandals. Pelias, hyper-sensitive to the possibility of one day encountering his one-sandaled nemesis, lasers in on this detail when Jason arrives in Iolcus:

But what will Pelias do about Jason? What Acrisius tried to do to Perseus by locking him up in a chest and tossing him out to sea? What Polydectes tried to do by having him go after Medusa? What Hera tried to do by tossing snakes into Heracles' crib? What Theseus almost did to himself by going after the Minotaur? In other words, will Pelias try to *kill* Jason, now that the oracle seems to be in the process of being fulfilled? That's what we expect him to do. And that's why he's not going to do it—or rather why the author of the story isn't going to *let* him do it: because it would be the predictable thing to do and he wants to do things differently than authors who came before him.

You notice I've used the phrase "author of the story." Up to now the heroes we've been looking at (Perseus, Heracles, and Theseus) lack a single literary work we can point to as *the* authoritative source for their respective myths. When we turn to Homer in the next two chapters, on the other hand, we'll encounter heroes we know primarily through his epics. The same goes for Jason: he too is best known to us through a single author. Homer's epics were composed around 750 BC, near the *beginning* of Greek history, despite dealing with heroes who fought the Trojan War *after* the heroes we've considered thus far went on their hero-quests. The epic we rely on most for the Jason story, the *Argonautica*, was composed around 250 BC, five hundred years *after* Homer, near the *end* of Greek history, despite dealing with a hero who went on his hero-quest *before* the heroes of Homer's epics fought the Trojan War.

That is why we're bothering to include Jason—and, by extension, an author who wrote hundreds of years after Homer did—in a book aiming to lead the reader up to Homer's doorstep. The author, Apollonius Rhodius, takes a self-consciously different approach to poetry than Homer did in several respects, and it's worth looking into, if for no other reason than to contrast him with Homer. He is writing in the period after the death of Alexander the Great (356-323 BC), who decides before he dies that what he needs to do is create a legacy for himself, not in Greece but in Egypt, because by this time Athens is less culturally prestigious, after the heyday of Pericles a century earlier. So he founds a city and names it after himself, Alexandria, which he does all he can to assure will be the new cultural capital, the new Athens.

Besides preserving the great works of the past, the librarians at Alexandria fancied themselves poets in their own right. It's how they sought to distinguish themselves from their Athenian predecessors.

Apollonius' Jason, then, is a different kind of hero. Rather than kill off the one-sandaled man when he shows up as he feared he would, Pelias has him undergo something similar to Heracles' and Theseus' labors but different from them in the sense of *why*. He will do so neither to prove his manhood to a king who enables his egoism to clear the way to pursue his mother (Perseus), nor to atone for the slaughter of his family (Heracles), nor to help his father deal with political rivals in Athens (Theseus), but to avoid the fulfillment of an oracle. Apollonius patterns Jason, that is, not as much on a previous hero as on Uranus, Cronus, and Zeus, fellow oracular fugitives.[71] With Jason we have come full circle: a hero who emulates the gods with respect to both the great deeds they achieve and the paranoia they succumb to.

Rather than kill Jason, then, Pelias is going to send him on a quest to the other end of the world to retrieve the Golden Fleece, the hide of a ram that rescued a boy named Phrixus about to be sacrificed to appease the gods, who in turn, upon reaching Colchis safely, sacrificed the ram to Poseidon[72] and hung it in a grove guarded by an insomniac dragon. Pelias doesn't expect Jason to be able to retrieve the Golden Fleece because he knows it can only be achieved by a legitimate hero and he doesn't know about Jason's heroic lineage, that he is a descendent, not of Zeus (as with Perseus and Heracles), nor of Poseidon (as with Theseus), but of Prometheus, one of the few Titans to help the Olympians in the Titanomachy and who, according to one mythic tradition, made the first human beings out of clay.[73]

What Prometheus is most famous for, however, is how much he *loves* human beings. He ascends the sky to visit Helius and when the latter isn't looking he ignites a torch from his eternal fire and brings it down to humans so they can plug in their laptops at Starbucks, making

---

[71] Granted, Pelias is trying to avoid *physical* annihilation (i.e., death), while Uranus and his descendants are avoiding *political* annihilation (i.e., usurpation), but the analogy still holds.

[72] Recalling Amalthea's sad fate as well as Minos' *refusal* to sacrifice the bull from the sea. Notice how the mythic associations are piling up at this stage in the evolution of the Greek hero.

[73] Which is interesting because in Latin the word *humanus* comes from the word *humus* meaning "soil" or, if you wish, "clay."

use of a natural element that symbolizes culture, civilization, and intelligence. The Olympics committee coopts this symbolism by transporting the perpetually lit torch from one community to another, representing at first the unification of all Greek communities, then expanding to encompass all communities in the world at large.

When Prometheus brings fire down from the sky, however, Zeus, the guy in charge upstairs, doesn't like the idea at all. He wants humans to be completely separate from the gods and the gods to leave them to their own devices. Prometheus, on the other hand, wants human beings not only to survive but to thrive. It's no coincidence that Jason, who exhibits an all-too-human sensitivity out of sync with the way heroism used to be done in the pre-Hellenistic heyday (which, by the way, is most assuredly *not* deterministically linked to the Jason myth by any means, but rather a reflection of the artistic sensibilities of Apollonius Rhodius' times) is the descendent not of Zeus or Poseidon but Prometheus, who despite helping Zeus in the Titanomachy has begun to really rile him.

Not only because of bringing fire from Olympus but also because he taught human beings how to cheat the gods by sacrificing to them the inferior parts of a victim while trying to fool them into believing they were its superior parts. Zeus, albeit not omniscient, knows precisely what Prometheus was up to but pretended to fall for his trick to justify punishing him by chaining him to a cliff far away in the Caucasus mountains so an eagle (symbolizing whom?) could come each day and peck at his side until it penetrated the skin, muscle, and fat down to his liver and eat it and return the next day, once the liver has grown back, to repeat the process, day after day, theoretically for eternity (he's ultimately freed by an ancestor of Heracles). And all because he loves human beings!

The Golden Fleece, then, is Jason's Medusa, his Nemean Lion, his Minotaur: rather than kill a wild beast he retrieves the hide of one that's already been killed by a child, hardly a heroic act in the old-school sense of the term. Compare the iconic images of Perseus killing Medusa, Heracles killing the Nemean lion, and Theseus killing the Minotaur with, well, whatever this is:

And yet, although he doesn't have to kill the way his predecessors did to prove his heroic mettle, Jason's heroism anticipates that of another hero who, albeit a great warrior in his own right, will be best known for the dangerous travels he will have to undergo: Odysseus. Jason's distant journey to retrieve the Golden Fleece will involve his own proprietary set of labors, which have an unmistakably Hellenistic quaintness about them. And yet, before going on his quest, he avoids making the same mistake Odysseus will make when he rejects the help of the gods at first until learning how indispensable it is to him. Rather, Jason gets help from the same goddess who has helped Perseus, Heracles, and Theseus in *their* quests: Athena, who appoints Argos (a descendant of Apollo) to build a ship—the Argo, named after him—that can talk, navigate, and prophesize, a proto-Siri:

Then there are the Argonauts ("Argo Sailors"), fifty heroes joining Jason on his journey, including Heracles and Theseus, which reminds us that although Perseus, great-grandfather of Heracles, is no longer around, Heracles, Theseus, and Jason are contemporaries. Several of the fathers of Trojan War heroes are also on board: Peleus (father of Achilles), Laertes (father of Odysseus), and Telamon (father of Ajax), providing a nice segue into the Homeric epics. We have something new here, though: heroes best known from other myths combined into a single story to accomplish a task requiring the critical mass that only their collective efforts can attain. The Argonauts, in other words, are the proto-Avengers, and the voyage of the Argo is the minor grass-court tournament before the Wimbledon of the Trojan War.

CHAPTER THIRTEEN

ILIAD[74]

The historical period of ancient Greece is inaugurated in the eighth century BC by the Homeric epics, a major cultural watershed. While no authoritative literary treatment is extant for the Perseus, Heracles, or Theseus myths we've considered thus far,[75] around 750 BC, seemingly out of nowhere, come the *Iliad* and the *Odyssey*, representing the gods of Olympus and the heroes of Greece and Troy by means of a highly developed diction, imagery, character, and plot construction that in fact *didn't* come out of nowhere, but rather as the culmination of a long tradition of oral epic reaching at least as far back as the Mycenaean Age.

How do we know about the stories of Perseus, Heracles, and Theseus? From ancient scholars who summarized the works of writers who have since been lost to us and whose summaries are thus all we know of their works. Homer, then, is uniquely important due to his historical seniority, but even more so due to the intrinsic value of his art. The ancient Greeks were not only familiar with Homer but took for granted his cultural centrality. They knew his epics through and through.

---

[74] Spoiler alert: in the final three chapters of this book we're going to learn a little about Homer himself, his epics, and some pertinent myths that immediately follow the Trojan War. Think of these chapters, however, less as an introduction to Homer *per se* (for that you would do well to consult W.A. Camps's *Introduction to Homer* [1980] or Mark W. Edwards's *Homer: Poet of the Iliad* [1990]) than as what the film industry refers to as a "teaser," which will hopefully push you over the edge to read the epics themselves.

[75] While there *is* an authoritative literary treatment for Jason, as we saw last chapter, it was published some five hundred years after Homer.

81

The Trojan War occurred in the Mycenaean Age. When Mycenaean civilization was destroyed by the "Sea Peoples,"[76] it resulted in a so-called Dark Age in which writing temporarily disappeared. Suddenly the Homeric epics emerge, still at a point where they're not written down yet but sung to an audience extemporaneously. But how can works so complex be improvised? Not everyone agrees on an answer. To deal with this "Homeric Question" (deemed important enough to be capitalized), Homerists until the 1930s tended to divide themselves into two camps. The Analysts argued that the *Iliad* and the *Odyssey* were hodgepodges, that different poets from different ages composed different parts of them and tacked them together. The Unitarians, on the other hand, argued that there was no way works so complex could have possibly been composed by a bunch of different people, that they had to be the product of one great genius.[77] A classicist named Milman Parry came along and crashed the party:

"You guys are fighting an unwinnable war," said Parry. "You're conceiving of the *Iliad* and the *Odyssey* as literature, as artworks originally written down. But guess what? They're *oral* works, sung out loud. It's only by studying people who compose works in the same way Homer did that we can gain some concrete insight into his methodology. And it just so happens that in Yugoslavia there are singers who essentially do what Homer did, compose extremely complex poetic works extemporaneously. I'm going to take a look."

And he did: in the 1930s he traveled to (what was still a nominally unified) Yugoslavia with his crew and did field research and because of his studies into how Homer did what he did, using the *guslars* (singers) of Yugoslavia as his analogue, he identified previously neglected aspects

---

[76] In other words, we don't know who they were. Maybe if we were talking about a modern group of people we would be calling them the "Air Peoples."

[77] Ignoring the fact that a collaborative venture like a film often involves several minds at work on different aspects of it.

of the mechanics of Homeric performance: sure Homer improvised his poems, but he didn't start out with a blank slate and come up with everything *ex vacuo*. He had certain themes and poetic phrases already in mind for types of situations that might arise in his narrative. These ready-made phrases, called formulae, allowed him to fill up a certain portion of a line of poetry while thinking of something new with which to fill the next part of the line or, if he was already at the end of a line, the first portion of the next line. In other words, Homer was the first freestyle rapper.

The backdrop of the *Iliad* is the Trojan War between the Greeks and Trojans, fought at Troy, on the west coast of Asia Minor, right across the Aegean from Greece. Did it actually take place? Until the middle 1800s it was routinely assumed that it hadn't, that it was a myth like any other. Until, that is, Heinrich Schliemann came along:

His father had read the *Iliad* to him as a child and whenever he took a break, little Heinrich would ask him questions that took for granted the historical reality of the Trojan War. His father would smile and tell him: "It's all made up, Heinrich, it's all fiction, like any other story I might read you." Schliemann, however, would have none of it: "No Daddy," he said, "one day I shall go over to Troy and prove that the Trojan War really took place." By his middle thirties he became successful enough at business to retire and devote himself wholeheartedly to looking for the site of the Trojan War. He eventually discovered it and then crossed the Aegean and discovered the site of Mycenae on the Greek mainland. Because of these achievements he's often referred to as the "father of modern (i.e., scientific) archaeology."

The Trojan War, then, *did* occur. As to *why* it occurred there's a traditional backstory, rooted in myth (get that straight: a mythical explanation for a real war) about the wedding of a mortal named Peleus and a sea-goddess named Thetis. At this wedding everyone's invited except for Eris, and it's obvious why she isn't invited: her name means "Strife." Why invite Strife to your wedding, right? Eris becomes so angry, however, that she crashes the wedding and throws a golden apple into the crowd with a label on it that says, "To the fairest":

Three goddesses fight over the golden apple like a foul ball at the World Series: Hera, Athena, and Aphrodite. There needs to be a decision made about who gets it but it's a tie so Zeus says, "I'm going to appoint a judge to determine which of you gets to keep it." Zeus appoints a young man named Paris to this task, a son of Priam, king of Troy,[78] the most handsome man in the world. Each of the three goddesses bribes Paris. Hera offers him what you would expect her to offer as queen of the gods in Olympus: political power. Equally predictably, Athena offers military ability. And Aphrodite offers Helen, the most beautiful woman in the world, so beautiful that later on (spoiler alert) she'll be referred to as "the face that launched a thousand ships." Guess which bribe Paris chooses.

---

[78] Suddenly Troy comes into the picture, linking western and eastern destinies the way the death of Minos' son Androgeus links Athens with Crete.

There's only one problem, though: Helen is married. Not only that, she's married to a *Greek*, to Menelaus, king of Sparta no less. Paris, then, needs to arrange to be brought over to Sparta, under the pretense of a peaceful get-together, so he can meet Helen and convince her to go along with him back to Troy, although it will involve a downgrade from queen of Sparta to princess of Troy. It works; she falls for him pretty hard:

Paris returns with Helen to Troy and they pay a visit to Priam, king of Troy. "Meet my new wife Helen," says Paris. Priam sees her and says, "Um, wait a minute, isn't that the wife of the king of Sparta? What are you doing with the [expletive] queen of Sparta?" And Paris says, "I won her in a contest." Then he goes into the story about Eris at the wedding of Peleus and Thetis and Priam asks how he could be so foolish as to accept a gift resulting from Strife throwing something into a crowd to generate strife, her specialty, but it goes in one ear and out the other. Menelaus, cuckolded by the prince of Troy, goes to his brother Agamemnon, king of Mycenae, tells him what has happened, and persuades him to declare war on Troy. Agamemnon persuades various kings throughout Greece to sail their own men on their own ships to Troy. Agamemnon is the nominal leader of the Greeks but their actual leader, their greatest warrior by far, is Achilles, as superior to any other Greek as Zeus is to any other Olympian. He resents Agamemnon for his merely symbolic power. Therein hangs a tale, the central conflict, in fact, of the *Iliad*: it's the anger of Achilles *toward* Agamemnon that is going to drive the epic forward,[79] and it's (spoiler alert) Achilles' overcoming of this anger that eventually enables the Greeks to win the war.

---

[79] In fact, "anger" is the very first word of the *Iliad*, as we'll see in the APPENDIX.

CHAPTER FOURTEEN

ODYSSEY

The Trojan War *officially* ends, though, with the stratagem of the Trojan horse. Odysseus, the most intelligent of the Greeks who travel to Troy,[80] comes up with the idea of building it and filling it with fifty or so Greek men. While it's still outside the walls of Troy, a putative Greek straggler informs the Trojans that they have given up on the war, that the Trojans are too formidable an enemy for them to continue fighting. Once, however, the Trojans drag the horse through the walls of Troy and celebrate their supposed war victory, getting drunk and falling asleep, the Greeks inside the horse sneak out in the middle of the night and let the rest of the army into Troy and turn what the Trojans believe to be a victory on their part into a defeat. There's an expression, "Beware of Greeks bearing gifts," and this is where it comes from.

Whereas the *telos*, or ultimate goal, of the *Iliad* consists of Achilles overcoming his anger (something *inside* of him), the *telos* of the *Odyssey* is for Odysseus to get home (something *outside* of him), which is more consistent with the sort of hero-quest we've been encountering so far (yet it also underscores the

---

[80] While Achilles' Homeric epithet is "swift-footed," reflecting the fact that he is fast (and, more generally, something *physical* about him), Odysseus' epithet is *polytropos*, which means "man of many turns," reflecting the fact that he's a great multi-tasker, can do many things at a time and very well (and, more generally, something *mental* about him). In other words, Odysseus is a gamer.

uniqueness of the *Iliad* in this respect). The *Odyssey*, then, is a *nostos-story*, dealing with the homecoming of a hero.[81] The home Odysseus will return to after the Trojan War is the island of Ithaka, where he is king. His wife Penelope is there waiting for him, lying to the suitors vying for her attention that as soon as she finishes the shroud she's weaving for Laertes, Odysseus' father, she will marry one of them. Each time she finishes it, though, she secretly destroys it and starts all over again:

As a war poem, most of the action of the *Iliad* consists of fighting. And except for a single, inconsequential scene, Homer contains all of the action of his poem within the conspicuously symmetrical limits of the Greek camp and Troy, on the horizontal plane, and Olympus and the Underworld, on the vertical plane. In the *Odyssey* it's the opposite situation: its story space is sprawled all over the place, reflecting the colonizing impulse of the eighth century BC, around the time the epic was composed. While in the *Iliad* you always have the sense that a god or goddess might swoop down to earth from Olympus without notice—given how close Olympus and the earth seem to be to each other—so in the Odyssey, no matter how much you root for Odysseus to get home to Penelope, you have the feeling that the harder he tries to do so, the more futile his journey becomes, the further apart he and Penelope seem to be from each other.

Indeed, there's a tension throughout the *Odyssey* that is analogous to when someone calls you and leaves a message on your voicemail but you're away and you get to your phone much later[82] and notice there are

---

[81] It's interesting that there's a basic term in ancient Greek that means "homecoming," not built from other words (you can combine all kinds of words and make pretty much any word-combinations you want from them) but a basic root-word meaning "homecoming," reflecting the extensive travel, trade, and colonization occurring in Archaic Greece.

[82] I fear there will come a day when most people reading this will scratch their heads as to what I could possibly mean by this.

two messages from the same person, the second message implying by its tone, "Oh, okay, if you don't want to call me." You get frustrated. You call them back and rather than pick it up themselves their voicemail does. What do you say? If you try to explain yourself it comes off as protesting too loudly. If you don't you might seem indifferent. That's how the *Odyssey* feels a lot of the time. Throughout the epic you feel Odysseus' frustration at really, really wanting Penelope to know he's going through all this stuff for her. He never dwells on power, on things like, "I want to be king of Ithaka again." He's not that kind of guy, he's not an Agamemnon. And so there's this wrenching tension throughout the *Odyssey* the same way there would be for you if you were doing all kinds of things for someone to help them out and they didn't even know it and, worse than that, thought you didn't care.

Then there are the suitors, the aristocratic men from various families on Ithaka, none of whom are kings but some of whom are sons or sons of sons of aristocrats who may have been kings in other areas, important men vying for marriage to Odysseus' wife. You have *that* tension too: Odysseus wanting Penelope to know he's on his way because he knows that otherwise she's going to end up marrying someone else as soon as Telemachus, their son, starts growing a beard. That's the pact they made before Odysseus left for the Trojan War: you get married to someone else if I don't come back by the time Telemachus (who was an infant at the time) has some stubble on his chin. Hence the delay-tactic on Penelope's part of weaving the shroud. She, of course, also wishes *Odysseus* knew what *she* was doing for *him*.

The greatest obstacle for Odysseus is Poseidon, god of the sea. It's not that he hates Odysseus as a hero or a person or a king or anything like that, not at all: he respects him, likes him, loves him, because Poseidon was staunchly on the side of the Greeks in the Trojan War.[83]

---

[83] Most of the Olympians take one side or another in the Trojan War, and their reasons for doing so are pretty straightforward. Hera was one of the two goddesses who got shunned in the Judgment of Paris, so of course she's going to be on the side of the Greeks. Athena is obviously going to be for the Greeks, more staunchly than any other Olympian. Poseidon is for the Greeks because he collaborated with Apollo in building the Trojan walls and wasn't worshipped enough by the Trojans to persuade him to be on their

Odysseus is one of the most prominent Greeks, so why is Poseidon Odysseus' Wicked Witch of the West? Because Odysseus—after coming up with the stratagem of the Trojan horse, getting credit for sealing the Trojan coffin, and beating out Ajax for the arms of Achilles (as we'll see in the next chapter)—starts feeling invincible, self-sufficient, indifferent to the gods, better even than Achilles because of his cool-factor, his having expended relatively little energy to come up with the idea that won the war rather than just a battle here and there, which was Achilles' forte.

Odysseus, then, gets such a big head that he makes it clear to the gods that he doesn't need their help anymore. He brags, for example, while leaving the island of the Cyclops Polyphemus, about his heroic lineage, flaunting his success after blinding him, who entreats Poseidon (his father) to punish Odysseus for his hubris.[84] No matter how great a hero Odysseus is, then, Poseidon teaches him a lesson: "Don't go thinking you're better than a human being. I don't care if you're part immortal: what that means to me and the other Olympians is that you're part mortal. I live with a bunch of immortals in Olympus. That's not special to us. What's special to us is that you're half *not* the thing we all are, and look at you thinking you're as good as we are."

That's the crux of Poseidon's anger and he takes it upon himself (via Aeolus, keeper of the winds, special effects coordinator) to punish Odysseus by causing a storm (which he's good at) so disastrous that although he gets within eye-shot of Ithaka, it blows him so far off course that it takes ten more years (the same number as the Trojan War itself) to finally get home. Odysseus' companions drop off one after another and

---

side. Apollo, on the other hand, takes the side of the Trojans, despite the Trojan wall incident, due to the fact that at the beginning of the *Iliad* Chryses, priest of Apollo, is dissed by Agamemnon, who refuses to hand over his daughter Chryseis when he walks from Troy to the Greek camp to ransom her. Artemis also takes the side of the Trojans, which is no surprise considering that she tends to be on the side of Apollo in general. Aphrodite, who won the contest of the golden apple, is of course going to favor Paris.

[84] The same quality of "overweening pride" exhibited by someone like Arachne, who challenges Athena to a weaving contest and gets turned into a spider because of her daring to do so, to overstep the bounds of being human, to refuse to play second-fiddle to the gods despite their less-than-perfect ways.

he is the only one left at the end of a journey on which he encounters one *Wizard of Oz*-type character after another, visits various communities that contrast in instructive ways with the Homeric audience's sense of what constitutes legitimate culture, such as the wild island Polyphemus lives on, whom Odysseus symbolically overcomes and who thereby becomes *his* Medusa:

The most interesting obstacles Odysseus encounters, however, are of a different kind: not wild creatures, as with the other heroes, but *female* characters who captivate him sexually, a type developed most fully centuries later with Medea in Apollonius Rhodius' *Argonautica* and Dido in Vergil's *Aeneid*. There's some irony here, of course: Odysseus' biggest challenges are not Nemean lions or Minotaurs but beautiful goddesses who can't get enough of him. Circe, for example, is a witch who uses her magical powers to seduce men in an overtly symbolic manner: when they become overwrought sexually she turns them into wild animals, the sort of creatures heroes are supposed to slay, not to become:

91

Before arriving at Circe's lair, Odysseus has been given a drug by Hermes so that he can avoid the fate of those who came before him, the subtext being that he can't do it on his own, that he needs Hermes' (and, in the bigger picture, the gods') help. Slowly but surely he's transcending his hubris. Circe tries to turn him into an animal like the others (or rather, to enable his turning himself into an animal) but it doesn't work. So, of course, she gets more into him and they have an affair but eventually he leaves.

He encounters another *femme fatale*, Calypso, a debilitatingly beautiful sea-goddess. A similar thing happens, however: he ends up hanging out with her for awhile but is eventually visited by Hermes, who informs him it's time stop the insanity, to go home to his wife Penelope:

Odysseus says his goodbyes to Calypso, whom he has fallen in love with (this is not a Circe figure), but he allows himself to recall that his wife is the one he loves most and he heads back to Ithaka. Not, however, before passing by the Sirens, sea-deities who sing so seductively that Odysseus has to have his men tie him down to the mast of his vessel so he won't do what everyone else tends to do, drown in the attempt to swim toward them:

Odysseus survives the Sirens' call and finally gets back to Ithaka. He still has his work cut out for him, though, because now he has to overcome the suitors who are after his wife and livelihood, and he does. Not before he lingers for awhile at his palace, though, disguised as a beggar, to find out which of the people who work at his palace have been true to Penelope and which haven't. He defeats the suitors and the disloyal workers with the help of his loyal son Telemachus, and he and Penelope are reunited:

CHAPTER FIFTEEN

AFTER TROY

Achilles dies when Paris shoots him with an arrow in the "Achilles heel":

It's his only vulnerable spot because it's where Thetis held him as an infant when she dipped him in the river Styx to make him immortal, the one place covered up by her hand when it went under:

Achilles doesn't die in the *Iliad* itself, however. The epic ends after Priam, king of Troy, ransoms Hector's corpse from Achilles. Achilles, then, dies at the hands of Paris, or rather at the *arrow* of Paris, which is significant because Paris, the "pretty-boy" of the Trojans, shoots Achilles with an arrow from a distance, the type of fighting perceived by the

Greeks to be less heroic than the hand-to-hand combat that real men engaged in.

Once Achilles is dead, both the Greeks and the Trojans fight over the arms wrought for him by Hephaestus after losing his first set on the battlefield once his BFF Patroclus (who couldn't stand watching Achilles sit out of the fighting due to his anger toward Agamemnon) went out to fight against the Trojans. Patroclus asked Achilles if he could enter the fray wearing his armor, the better to scare the Trojans with, and Achilles agreed to it as long as he retreated once he reached the Trojan walls. Patroclus disobeyed his wishes, however, and kept on fighting and was killed by Hector who, upon discovering it wasn't Achilles he killed but Patroclus, took the armor away. Thetis went up to Olympus and asked Hephaestus for new armor, which she then delivered to Achilles:

The Greeks decide that this famous armor should be awarded to the second greatest warrior after Achilles. There's debate, however, as to who that is. Does it mean the greatest fighter *per se*, the greatest brawler (protégé of Ares), or the greatest strategist (protégé of Athena)? Most of the Greeks assume that Ajax will win the armor, the man now most capable of killing the greatest number of people. They also know that Ajax and Achilles were great friends, close enough for Ajax to be the one to dare to try to persuade Achilles to return to the fray after sulking away with his Myrmidons after his fight with Agamemnon over his harsh treatment of the priest of Apollo. Their friendship is portrayed on a famous vase by Exekias that depicts Achilles (left) and Ajax (right) playing a game of dice with each other:

Odysseus too competes for the armor, however, making the case that *he's* the second best after Achilles because of his superior intellect and unmatched cruelty to the Trojans. Because of this speech, Odysseus, rather than the less rhetorically adept Ajax, is awarded Achilles' arms.

This brings us to a play called *Ajax* by Sophocles (496-406 BC), in which the hero goes insane because of his anger and sadness about this decision. As a result, he does something reminiscent of Heracles: he goes on a killing spree. The details are different, however: he thinks he's killing a bunch of Greek warriors but actually kills a bunch of sheep. To understand what happens next, we need to realize how all-important reputation is to the ancient Greek hero. What other people think about him, earning and maintaining their respect, is everything to him, no less so than for a Scorsese character. Ajax, then, is ridiculed for his behavior and it penetrates so deeply that he falls onto his sword in embarrassment and shame, the preparation for which moment is poignantly captured by Exekias in yet another great vase-painting, a tragic companion-piece to the more jovial (yet, unless I'm reading in, ominous) scene above:

We conclude with the story of Agamemnon, nominal king of the Greek expedition to Troy, in the aftermath of the Trojan War and his arrival home which (spoiler alert) ends up badly for him. Agamemnon is a son of Atreus, member (as alluded to in the ZEUS, HERA chapter) of one of the most cursed families in Greek myth, at the tail-end of several generations of events leading up to Agamemnon also being cursed. Not only was the Trojan War central to Greek myth but so were the homecomings of various Greek heroes, the two most important of which are Odysseus and Agamemnon, the latter being the protagonist of an eponymous tragedy by Aeschylus (525-456 BC), the first of three plays that comprise the *Oresteia*, the only extant trilogy from ancient Greece.

Agamemnon, after ten years in Troy, comes back home to Mycenae, one of the two most important centers of Greek prehistory (the other is Crete). His wife Clytemnestra, queen of Mycenae, has been waiting ten years for him to get home and stands in stark contrast to Penelope (who has been waiting twenty years for Odysseus to get home): two wives, one staunchly loyal, the other quite the opposite. Indeed, while Agamemnon is gone, not only is Clytemnestra not pining over her husband, she's having an affair with a man named Aegisthus, which the audience may or may not believe is justified based on what Agamemnon did to make her angry enough to actually kill him.[85]

Agamemnon arrives home with Cassandra, daughter of King Priam but now a war-slave who possesses a strange sort of prophetic power: she prophesizes accurately but no one believes her, punishment from Apollo for failing to be impressed enough by the power of prophesy he gave her to succumb to him. Agamemnon, then, by arriving with Cassandra, is adding insult to injury as far as Clytemnestra is concerned. This is where the story starts getting psychologically interesting. Clytemnestra pretends, quite convincingly, that she's happy Agamemnon has made it home, and Aeschylus makes it clear to the audience that deception is involved here, that she's doing all she can to fool him into thinking this. He goes into the house with Clytemnestra and Cassandra starts

---

[85] See footnote 59.

prophesizing that Agamemnon is doomed, but consistent with her curse, no one believes what she's saying (other than the audience, of course).

Then we hear a cry from inside the house and Clytemnestra comes out drenched in blood, inducing us to recall—and to put a different spin on—the fact that just before Agamemnon had gone into the house, Clytemnestra had symbolically lain a red carpet out for him to walk over. When she walks out bloody like this, the audience is not surprised it has missed out on seeing the murder of Agamemnon because the Athenians had a custom that you avoid showing murders on stage, for ethical reasons but also to maintain decorum, to leave such things to the imagination of the audience:[86]

I'm especially fond of French painter Pierre-Narcisse Guérin's 1822 painting in which he takes the imaginative leap of bringing us inside of Agamemnon's house the moment before the murder of the king. Guérin has Aegisthus goading Clytemnestra on, who looks more tentative about the idea than Aeschylus' own words might lead us to suspect. A fine pre-modern piece of tribute art:[87]

---

[86] Early Hollywood films observed the same custom until certain films, most notorious of which was 1967's "Bonnie and Clyde" (which seems tame by today's standards) obliterated it and Quentin Tarantino stomped on its grave.

[87] One can imagine him saying to her, "Let me get this straight: Helen, queen of Troy, is important enough to fight a war for, but Iphigenia, princess of Mycenae, isn't important enough not to sacrifice? What are you waiting for?"

The second play in the *Oresteia* trilogy is the *Libation Bearers*. Now that Agamemnon is dead, his son Orestes, after whom the trilogy is named, comes along, representing the next generation of blood-guilt in this mortal counterpart to the Succession Myth of Uranus, Cronus, and Zeus. He wants to avenge his father by killing his mother. He and his sister Electra get together and plot the murder:

Orestes kills Clytemnestra and Aegisthus. But now what? How long will this age-old vicious cycle of revenge last? At the end of the play, Orestes is driven insane out of guilt for his crime, exhibiting the agony one with a conscience undergoes when he or she ends someone else's life. This is Greek tragedy: *consciences* are involved; otherwise you don't have tragic characters but stick-figures who kill indiscriminately. Orestes is chased by the Furies, whose role is to punish human beings for familial blood-guilt:

The third and final play of the *Oresteia* is the *Eumenides*, the name given to the Furies once they're transformed at the end of the play into positive spirits (which is what their name means)[88] rather than negative ones. Orestes goes to the Oracle at Delphi to find out what to do to protect himself against the Furies:

---

[88] As with Cronus, their very name requires a spoiler alert. Which raises a bigger point: the Greeks didn't care about spoilers. While they appreciated suspense, it was not because they didn't know what was going to happen next in the story (they did), but because they were curious about how authors would generate said suspense differently than authors who came before them.

Apollo (right) tells Orestes (center) to go to Athens to request that Athena (left) put an end once and for all to the intergenerational blood-lust.[89] But what is that object Orestes clings to? The *omphalos*, the stone rejected by Cronus that landed at Delphi, establishing it as the center of the universe Apollo astutely associated himself with to become the Olympian most relevant to the post-mythic world. Orestes clings to it before leaving for Athens to seek justice in a real-world court of law. Zeus is nowhere to be found.

---

[89] Apollo, in other words, delivers a PSA for the Athenian law courts as the place to go to solve everything in a fair, equitable manner, as well as for Athens as the place to go to escape from Mycenae the way Theseus escaped from Crete.

APPENDIX[90]

THE FIRST TWO LINES OF THE ILIAD

Ancient Greek and Latin are often referred to as "dead languages," as opposed to "live languages," that is, languages still in use today, by living people. But what about when someone reads out loud to someone else the first line of the *Iliad*? Isn't that *using* language as well? Indeed it is: the reader is communicating with the listener no differently—from the standpoint of the listener's experience—than if the reader were Homer himself: the words are processed identically in the listener's mind in either case, and in that sense the language of Homer is still no less alive than the language we speak in our everyday lives, maybe even more so.

Ancient Greek and Latin are highly inflected languages. In the process of simplification inherent in their developing into so-called "common" versions of a more complex original tongue, the most conspicuous tradeoff is a reduction in inflectional complexity for an increase in word-order constraint. Once case-endings drop off the end of nouns, for example, their syntactic baggage is shifted to the realm of

---

[90] This is the transcript of a lecture called "In Praise of 'Dead' Languages" I delivered at San Diego State University on April 30, 2015, as part of the "Classics & Humanities Today" lecture series. The talk was accompanied by Powerpoint slides, the content of which should be pretty clear from their context. Where it's most difficult to get a sense of the original experience, however, is when it gets to a video of an orchestral performance by Anna Fedorova of Rachmaninoff's Second Piano Concerto that I played and replayed a few times to get a certain point across. The video, as of this writing, is located at the following URL: https://www.youtube.com/watch?v=rEGOihjqO9w, but I can't guarantee it will always be. As of 8/15/15 it has 4,220,241 views, however, so I assume that barring copyright issues (which is unfortunately very conceivable) it should continue to be online. If not, the basic point I'm trying to make, again, should be somewhat apparent from the context, and even if it weren't, I should hope including the lecture as the appendix to this book would still be justified overall, especially since the first two lines of the *Iliad* figure so prominently in it. The twofold thesis of this talk is that the ancient languages are every bit as alive as the literature they make available to those who can read them, and that because said literature is very alive indeed, learning the ancient languages is worth every precious hour of effort we put into it. Those who are not much interested in languages *per se* might wish to skip this section, in which case thanks for joining me thus far. Those who are interested in languages might find it worthwhile.

word order: rather than saying "canis mordit virum" or, if we wish, "virum mordit canis," we say "dog bites man" but *not* "man bites dog," which would be incorrect. The reason the latter would be incorrect is that—since by dropping case-endings word-order takes on a new prominence, picks up the slack from what used to be signified through the endings of words—the relationship between the word "dog" and the word "man" is no longer apparent the way the one between "canis" and "virum" is.

In the sentence, "virum mordit canis," the *–um* ending of "virum" tips me off as to what sort of word I might expect to encounter, *syntactically speaking*, in its future. On the other hand, in the sentence "canis mordit virum," the *–is* ending of "canis" points me in a different direction than the "virum" at the beginning of the previous sentence did. And, I submit to you, this *matters*. It matters because it reveals something the language, if we let it, is doing to us on a level different from the purely conceptual level on which the two aforementioned sentences operate more or less identically, when we deal exclusively with the information conveyed without concern for the way it's conveyed, the process we undergo as we let it work on us that way.

So why the dead language stigma? The fact is that, all other things being equal, the ancient languages are by far *more* alive than modern English, primarily because of their highly inflected nature, providing them, at least in poetry, with a stylistic edge over their modern counterparts: the freedom of the poet to place his words pretty much anywhere he or she wishes to in a given line of verse, and thus to give palpable meaning to Homer's epithet: *winged words*, to the *kinetic* dimension of words, their ability to travel from speaker to listener, from poet to audience.

In this sense, the language of Homer would only be dead if we lacked the knowledge required to make sense of the marks on the page we call Greek letters, and how they're combined in various ways to express ideas, representations of the sorts of events previously conveyed exclusively through visual art. By setting these word-pictures in motion, Homer becomes, among other things, the first cinematic artist, and his epics the first movies, employing what we draw from film vocabulary to refer to as the close-up, the long shot, and the transition between them called decomposition, animating the proto-cinematic visual art of Bronze Age, pre-Homeric Greece.

I began studying Latin in the Fall of 1988. While it's probably what should be embarrassingly nerdy to admit, I remember getting a kind of visceral thrill out of realizing that a noun could be put into a certain case that indicated it was in one sort of relationship to the verb rather than another. That simple relationship between verb and, in this case, accusative noun was a revelation to me, for whom the English sentence "I see the dog" never induced me to suspect that there was something going on with the word "dog" within it that was different than what would be going on with it if it were the dog who was doing the seeing. And why *would* this occur to me? "I see the dog." "The dog sees me." "Dog" in either case is identical, right? Wrong. They merely *look* identical but because they function differently in each respective sentence they are therefore *ipso facto* different. And here, on the first day of Latin class, I learn that words that function differently the way "dog" and "dog" do in the example just given tend also to *look* different in Latin. What a revelation!

Speaking of dogs, I'd like to begin with an example of one type of advantage of being able to read a so-called dead language such as ancient Greek or Latin in the original. It concerns Odysseus' dog Argos, who, in Book 17 of the *Odyssey*, despite his master having been away for twenty years, recognizes him the way no human is able to do (Euryclea's recognition of Odysseus' scar is cheating). In this case we'll be considering a single word, **nosphin**, which is translated by the LSJ as "aloof, apart, afar, away" and in the Argos scene is used in connection with Odysseus for only the third, and final, time in the epic. In its first use, Odysseus describes to the Phaeacians an experience he has had on his journey to the Underworld:

οἵη δ' Αἴαντος ψυχὴ Τελαμωνιάδαο
νόσφιν ἀφειστήκει, κεχολωμένη εἵνεκα νίκης,
τήν μιν ἐγὼ νίκησα δικαζόμενος παρὰ νηυσὶ
τεύχεσιν ἀμφ' Ἀχιλῆος: ἔθηκε δὲ πότνια μήτηρ.

Only the soul of Telamonian Ajax
νόσφιν stood away, angry because of the victory
that I had over him being judged by the ships
for the armor of Achilles given to him by his mother.
(11.543-546)

For Odysseus' second encounter with **νόσφιν**, the long-suffering hero, disguised as a beggar, is on the receiving end of a comment made by the goatherd Eumaeus about a man the knowledge of whose presence the poet allows us to share with the audience:

ἀλλά μ' Ὀδυσσῆος πόθος αἴνυται οἰχομένοιο.
τὸν μὲν ἐγών, ὦ ξεῖνε, καὶ οὐ παρεόντ' ὀνομάζειν
αἰδέομαι: πέρι γάρ μ' ἐφίλει καὶ κήδετο θυμῷ:
ἀλλά μιν ἠθεῖον καλέω καὶ **νόσφιν** ἐόντα.

But longing for Odysseus, who is gone, seizes me.
I am ashamed, stranger, to refer to the missing man by name,
for he loved and cared about me in his heart:
So I call him my esteemed friend although he is **νόσφιν**.
(14.144- 147)

Thus, **νόσφιν** is a word that both Odysseus uses to represent a certain spatial relationship between Ajax and himself in the Underworld and Eumaeus uses to represent a certain spatial relationship between Odysseus and himself on Ithaka. In both cases **νόσφιν** is being used to represent the profound emotional dynamic between Odysseus and another character.

This brings us to Odysseus' third and final encounter with **νόσφιν**, which will help us both to shed more light, albeit retrospectively, on the meanings of its first two uses and enrich our understanding of the particular meaning of its third use:

106

ἔνθα κύων κεῖτ' Ἄργος, ἐνίπλειος κυνοραιστέων.
δὴ τότε γ', ὡς ἐνόησεν Ὀδυσσέα ἐγγὺς ἐόντα,
οὐρῇ μέν ῥ' ὅ γ' ἔσηνε καὶ οὔατα κάββαλεν ἄμφω,
ἆσσον δ' οὐκέτ' ἔπειτα δυνήσατο οἷο ἄνακτος
ἐλθέμεν: αὐτὰρ ὁ νόσφιν ἰδὼν ἀπομόρξατο δάκρυ,
ῥεῖα λαθὼν Εὔμαιον, ἄφαρ δ' ἐρεείνετο μύθῳ:
Εὔμαι', ἦ μάλα θαῦμα, κύων ὅδε κεῖτ' ἐνὶ κόπρῳ.
καλὸς μὲν δέμας ἐστίν, ἀτὰρ τόδε γ' οὐ σάφα οἶδα,
εἰ δὴ καὶ ταχὺς ἔσκε θέειν ἐπὶ εἴδεϊ τῷδε,
ἦ αὔτως οἷοί τε τραπεζῆες κύνες ἀνδρῶν
γίνοντ': ἀγλαΐης δ' ἕνεκεν κομέουσιν ἄνακτες.

There lay the dog Argos, quite full of dog ticks.
Just then, as he noticed Odysseus coming near,
he wagged his tail and dropped both his ears,
but after that no longer had the strength to come closer
to his master. Then, looking νόσφιν, Odysseus wiped away a tear,
easily evading Eumaeus' notice, and immediately asked him:
"Eumaeus, it's very strange this dog lies on a dung pile.
His form is fine, but I don't know, at least don't know it clearly,
whether he was also fast at running, to match this shape of his,
or ran the same way as the kind that are table dogs of men,
whose masters take care of them for show."
(17.300-310)

What does it mean for Odysseus to be looking **νόσφιν** before wiping away his tear? The word is being used here as an adverb rather than, as it sometimes is, a preposition. And yet the meaning is far from unambiguous, as corroborated by two alternate readings (**ἰὼν** and **ἐὼν**) for the participle **ἰδὼν**,

ἐλθέμεν· αὐτὰρ ὁ νόσφιν ἰδὼν ἀπομόρξατο δάκρυ,
ῥεῖα λαθὼν Εὔμαιον, ἄφαρ δ' ἐρεείνετο μύθῳ·   305

279 ἠὲ βάλῃ a d P¹   281 φρονέοντι ●   282 ὑπολήψομαι p Pal.   286 ἀποπλῆσαι Clem. Al. strom. vi. 2. 12   289 φέροντες ●: φυτεῦσαι L³   291 δ' ὁ R¹: ἄνθ' ὁ Cocondrius Rhet. gr. viii. 792. 5   293 εἰς codd.   294 ᾦχ. codd.   295 πτῶκας R⁹U³, γρ. Br V⁴   296 ὀδυσῆος ● f j k ed. pr. : -οιο ὀδυσῆος g H³   299 δμῶες ἀναγκαῖοι E. M. 530. 44 (ἀνάγκη schol. Ω 164) = ω 210   κοπρήσοντες k M² P² Pˀ: -ίσσοντες p U²: κοπρίσοντες vulg.: κοπρήσονται Pal. (-ίσ-R²)   302 κάββαλεν c ● f r Eust.: κάμβαλεν cet.   304 ἰὼν ● L⁵L⁵: ἐὼν R¹   ἐπεμόρξατο o   305 μῦθον g Eust.

neither of which works, however, due to the fact that Odysseus has recently been described as being close (ἐγγὺς ἐόντα) to Argos. ἰδὼν, then, will have to do, but how?

To be **νόσφιν**, whether within or outside of the same physical proximity, is one thing, but to *look* **νόσφιν** is something else entirely: not a being **νόσφιν** but a *doing* **νόσφιν**, so that **νόσφιν** represents, not the physical distance between two men, nor the absence of one man from the location of another, but rather a kind of combination of the two: a wistful staring into a space both empty yet filled with memories—of Ajax and Eumaeus, two characters whose relationship to Odysseus is sufficiently intense to suggest that their association with the first two instances of **νόσφιν** is not merely coincidental but rather increases the poignancy of the scene by associating it with two equally significant experiences whose impact was to no small degree generated by the use of **νόσφιν** to express a comparably paradoxical sense of physical absence and emotional presence.

The fact that **νόσφιν** is used in connection first with Ajax and then with Eumaeus suggests that when it's used for its third time in connection with Argos we're justified in recalling its first two uses and acknowledging their contribution to the already profound emotional impact of the scene. It's only by noticing the occurrence of **νόσφιν** in each of these three scenes as a distinctive verbal event that we're able to make this connection between Ajax, Eumaeus, and Argos, which is denied to us when we use a translation unless the translator in question is careful to make sure that each time the word occurs it's rendered by the exact same word, to convey to the perceptive reader of the translation that this particular correspondence is occurring. With a poem of more than 12,000 lines, however, doing so for all or even most of the words we encounter in the text is unrealistic to expect.

So that's one type of advantage of reading Homer in the original: the ability to detect the repetition of specific words throughout the epic and to contextualize them and find meaning in their recurrent uses. You'll notice, however, that the word we've been considering thus far, **νόσφιν**, is an *uninflected* word, the significance of whose representation within the *Odyssey* is limited to *when,* and in conjunction with what other words, it occurs. But now I'd like to consider a different sort of advantage of reading Homer—and, by extension, so-called dead languages in general—in the original, which concerns not uninflected but rather *inflected* words. For while a translator might conceivably pull off a translation that manages to duplicate the repetition of every uninflected word in the *Iliad* and *Odyssey* (although it's highly unlikely), to attempt to do so for every *inflected* word, on the other hand, would be futile, given certain inherently distinctive grammatical differences between ancient Greek and modern English.

Back to Latin class. It wasn't long before I started thinking of the Latin sentence as a kind of jigsaw puzzle, the pieces of which fit snugly together by virtue of their relationship to each other. I was hooked. I couldn't wait to get to more complex types of sentences, where not only words but also groups of words can be combined into discrete units of meaning that are themselves combined with other words and groups of words. I couldn't wait to go to Latin class. I was a music student, so I couldn't wait to go to music theory class either, but Latin was special in a different way: it was making me look differently at something I had been using all my life, language, but was now becoming more conscious about, the way I was conscious about music. In fact, I soon realized that there was quite a bit of overlap between language and music. After all, they're both ways to communicate, and in both cases one does so by combining their elements into groups that mean more than the sum of their parts: words into clauses in the case of language, tones into chords in the case of music.

Take a look at this woman in the photo on the screen:

Can you tell what she's feeling? Does she look sad or happy? What if I told you she was not as much sad or happy as *anxious*? Anxious for what? For something to happen. What? For something to change into something else. For what to change? Music. She's listening to music. And at this moment she anticipates that where it is right now is not where it will be very soon. And when it gets to where she knows it will go next she looks like this:

Now how does she look? Sad or happy? What if I told you she was not as much sad or happy as *relieved*? Relieved by what? By the aforementioned change taking place. First we see anxiety, then relief. Are you curious about what the music is from one moment to the next, what the music is that makes her anxious and that dispels her anxiety, transports her into a state where she is moved so much by what happens in the music that she closes her eyes like this, to feel what has happened so fully that it induces her to surrender to her sense of hearing and temporarily to shut out her sense of sight? **[play the video of the second movement of Rachmoninoff's 2nd piano concerto]**[91]

Did you feel that? It's that threshold between one moment and the next—what in musical parlance is referred to as the transition between the dominant chord and the tonic chord—that I'd like us to focus on for a while. In the key of C,[92] the dominant chord consists of G, B, and D, as you see here, numerically represented by 5, 7, and 2, that is, the fifth, seventh, and second tones of this particular key signature.

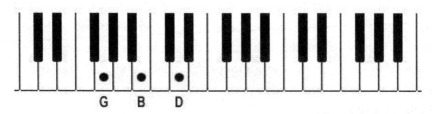

In the key of C, the B, just below C, gravitates toward C itself, the next key up, the D gravitates toward E, the next key up, and G, as the dominant tone of the key signature, is already at rest and thus wants to stay where it is.

---

[91] URL: https://www.youtube.com/watch?v=rEGOihjqO9w (as of 8/15/15)
[92] The movement is in a different key than C: I'm just using this as the clearest example.

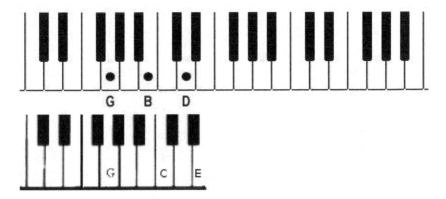

Let's play that part of the second movement of Rachmoninoff's 2nd piano concerto again, but this time I'm going to stop at the dominant chord, just before the resolution referred to occurs. But we're not going to let it resolve just yet: we're going to stop at the dominant, before the woman closes her eyes in bliss at having resolved to the tonic chord. See how it makes you feel **[play again but stop at 12:52]** You feel how you want it to progress to the next chord, so you, like this woman, can close your eyes and surrender to the music? Until that point you're not at ease but anxious for it to get there. Finally, let's let the dominant resolve to the tonic, and pay attention to how you feel this time. **[play again and allow to resolve to tonic]** Today I would like to suggest that just as a dominant chord points to a tonic chord that, once reached, satisfies our expectation for it to do so in a pleasurable way, so does—or at least can, under the right conditions—an accusative noun point to a transitive verb with the same sense of delicious inevitability.

Consider the first word of the *Iliad*, μῆνιν, transliterated into Roman script as **menin**, which is usually translated into English as "anger" or "rage," as in the four most popular translations of the *Iliad*:

RAGE:
Sing, Goddess, Achilles' rage, (Lombardo)

Rage—Goddess, sing the rage of Peleus' son Achilles (Fagles)

SING, goddess, the anger of Peleus' son Achilleus (Lattimore)

Anger be now your song, immortal one,
Akhilleus' anger, doomed and ruinous, (Fitzgerald)

In these four renderings, all but Lattimore place "anger" or "rage" at the beginning of the line, reflecting its initial-position placement in the original. The idea is that by doing this, the three translators are duplicating the first word of the original Homeric text. And insofar as all that matters is the stem of a word, its conceptual component, this is perfectly true. If, however, we choose to notice that **menin** is in a particular case and that the ending of the word, its grammatical component, reflects this fact, then we might not be satisfied with "anger" or "rage" as substitutes for **menin**. But why *should* we notice this fact? Does it really tell us anything worth bothering with?

menin means "anger" or "rage," as our four translators would have us believe, but only in the sense that a dominant chord in the key of C means G. But doesn't it also mean B and D? Indeed. In fact, without B and D, G would lack a sense of direction, depend on another tone to appear to establish its relationship to it, determine how it's to function at this particular moment in the piece. That's what's going on when we say that **menin** means "anger": to do so betrays an exclusive focus on the word's stem and an indifference to its ending, the **v** that reveals it's in the accusative case. If we're merely concerned with the *idea* of the word rather than how it works in its sentence, then a translation is fine (well, not really, but for different reasons). But if we also care about the way the word is tailored to its particular context in the sentence it belongs to, suddenly knowing G is no longer enough: we want to know if the G is tonic, dominant, or perhaps even some other degree of a new key we're about to transpose into.

menin is in the accusative case. Since it's not preceded by a preposition it's probably the direct object of the verb. But what will the verb be that results in the resolution of the accusative noun it generates? What tense will it be in? Will it be negated? We don't yet know. Our familiarity with, and internalization of the syntactic force of, the direct object makes us either wonder these things on a conscious level or more likely feel in our gut a semantic potentiality we've come to associate with the direct-object accusative. We're opening ourselves up to a certain type of meaning denied to us when we're wearing our stem-goggles, to the fact of how much more untranslatable the word becomes by incorporating it into our understanding of what is being said in the original. This serves to shift our focus from translation to reading the text directly, to allowing ourselves to process the words in real time, to let them work on us the way music works on us and with no less indifference to being able to translate what we're experiencing into some other medium, in the case of language into a different language, in the case of music onto a different instrument.

But even more, it shifts our focus from a synchronic to a diachronic perspective on **menin**, induces us to attend to its temporal force, to the way it makes us curious about how it will fit into the rest of the sentence *qua* isolated accusative, inviting our at least subconscious inquiry into its relationship to the verb, whether or not whatever insight we derive from it will shed light on, say, what the verb is likely to be. The direction this connotational process takes is less salient here than the manner in which our capacity to incorporate it into our understanding of the text opens up to us an otherwise untrodden heuristic avenue that yields a completely different type of meaning than what we would otherwise be paying attention to. It unlocks the poem's meaning to the faculty of curiosity about the future.

Otherwise we accept the supposed equivalence of **menin** and "anger," willfully ignoring the fact that while **menin** triggers an association with **menis**, its nominative counterpart, "anger" only triggers associations with *other words*, having bypassed whatever grammatical associations it might have were it, like **menin**, to be committed to a given morphological status. But it isn't. And therein lies the essential difference, from a hermeneutic standpoint, between highly inflected languages and hardly (or not at all) inflected languages and their correspondingly more or less grammatically differentiated forms.

menin implies the existence of, and deploys a relationship between, poet and audience, the real-world participants in the narrative. It also anticipates the existence of a so far unidentified transitive verb, of which **menin** will be the direct object, and the subject of said verb. Thus, **menin** operates on the mind in two distinct temporal dimensions simultaneously, requiring in poet and audience alike a capacity to absorb both the fact of their mutual existence at the farthest extremes of the communicative process and our uncertainty about the precise identity of the verb and subject that have yet to emerge.

So far we have only looked at the first word of the *Iliad*. When the second word, **aeide** (ἄειδε), enters the picture, it also operates in these two dimensions simultaneously, only now our identification of poet and audience as narrative agents is merely corroborated rather than expanded upon: the subject of the verb may conceivably be the audience-member *qua* addressee or someone else not yet mentioned, thereby creating the *potential* for an expansion of narrative agency without committing to whether or not it will occur. When **aeide** (ἄειδε) follows **menin**, the sentence comes alive for us: the imperative "sing" engages us differently than the syntactically ambiguous "RAGE" did, to which we'll now return, for comparison's sake:

RAGE:

What expectations does this word generate? Its syntactic indeterminism leaves open-ended where the poet might wish to go next: the word might be in the nominative, accusative, or vocative case: our uncertainty on this score prevents us from initiating a specific string of expectations of the sort we harbored when we encountered accusative-tinged anger in the original. We see this provocatively punctuated word in scare capitals and, despite Lombardo's best intentions, we don't know what to think. It's the first word of the most popular translation of the *Iliad* and it mystifies us. The colon asks us to look ahead but we don't know what to expect, what to look forward *to*. Is a term about to be defined, described, explained, put under a microscope?

Lombardo means well: he places "RAGE" at the beginning of his translation of the *Iliad* to respect Homer's decision to begin his epic with this particular word in the original Greek. The problem is: this *isn't* the same word as the word the poet chose to use, but rather a grammatically neutral facsimile thereof, preserving its conceptual value but ignoring its syntactic status within the rest of the sentence. And because of this, our relationship to Lombardo's rage is different from our relationship to Homer's **menin**: whereas the former leaves us in the dark as to what to expect next, the latter points us toward the transitive verb it will serve as the direct object of. So when **aeide** appears, our uncertainty about which verb will fill the syntactic slot formed by our **menin**-induced curiosity has been dispelled—but *not* about the particular subject of the verb, which the next word, **thea** (θεὰ), reveals to us even as it expands the narrative agency of the epic, adding Muse to poet and audience, interdependent representatives of the real world within which real people are sitting in real seats listening to the poet delivering to them the narrative in real time.

Let us now bring meter into the picture. The final syllable of **thea** falls just before the caesura, the main point *within* the line where the poet pauses to take a breath. A caesural pause is more or less significant depending on its semantic context. While determining whether or not a given pause is significant can be more or less subjective, in some cases more than others we have greater justification for considering it to be significant. I submit that the present instance—which happens to be the first caesura of extant western verbal narrative—constitutes one such case: having reached the point where, on the ontological level, poet and audience and Muse have been introduced into the narrative and where, on the syntactical level, the transitive verb governing **menin** and its subject have been revealed, we arrive at a point where our curiosity is funneled into a single, overriding preoccupation: the **menis** itself. Whose is it?

Our answer comes with the fourth and fifth words of line 1, **Peleiadeo Achilleos** (Πηληϊάδεω Ἀχιλῆος), which introduce into the story two more characters—one from the past and one from the present, one mortal and the other semi-mortal—who, along with the Muse, operate in the fictional world rather than (as in the case of poet and audience) the real world, and thus complete the typology of narrative agency established by the first five words of the epic and to which all subsequent narrative agents will conform: the poet channels for the audience the Muse's song about mortal, semi-mortal, and immortal characters who will perform actions within the story.

We are ready for the second line, just one word of it. But the poet and audience whose existence was brought into being in and through the first word of the poem take a metrically subsidized pause at the end of the first line—as is customary at the beginnings and endings of lines as well as within them at caesurae—and our curiosity takes a kind of hiatus as well: whereas before the caesura we wondered whose **menis** we were dealing with, now that we know the answer we're not sure where the poet will go next: will he say something about the anger, the singing, the goddess, Peleus, Achilles, or introduce something new into the narrative?

At the beginning of line 2 we have our answer: we learn something about the *nature* of the **menis**, that it's a particularly *destructive* anger, as represented by the adjective **oulomene** (οὐλομένη), in the accusative case like **menin** and ending in **v** to reveal its syntactic correspondence to **menin** (not to mention the phonetic correspondence between the final five letters of the two words, which also slips through the cracks of translations). Through the vehicle of first-position placement the poet in effect juxtaposes **oulomenen** over **menin** as though the former were less an attribute of the latter than part and parcel of it, more explicitly and inseparably than through ordinary attribution yet different enough from it to call attention to it as a quality in its own right. As we have seen, translators of the *Iliad* tend to make a conspicuous effort to underscore the thematic centrality of **menis** by duplicating in their version its initial-position status. **menis** is not the first word of the *Iliad*, however, but **menin** is, and, from the standpoint of the sort of syntactical meaning we've been concerning ourselves with today, this makes all the difference.

In perhaps the most famous theoretical treatise on translation theory, *After Babel: Aspects of Language and Translation*, George Steiner points out that it's the ability of a given language, through grammatical means, to point into the future at things that have yet to occur that, if anything, constitutes an advantage over languages, such as certain Native American ones, that lack this capacity. Surprisingly, however, when Steiner gets more specific about precisely what aspects of grammar he's referring to, he identifies future tense verbs as the most formidable transmitters of potential reality. He doesn't go far enough, though: a future verb expresses futurity on only one level of the narrative, the story, but there's an equally important level, what we've been paying attention to today, the discourse, that pertains to, not the events within the fictional world, as the former does, but rather events within the real world of poet and audience.

To illustrate this distinction let's consider a famous amphora by Exekias from around 530 BC, depicting Achilles and Ajax playing dice.[93] Notice how the heroes bend over as they play, suggesting an intense devotion to the game on both of their parts. This bending over occurs within the context of the narrative depicted on the vase. That's the story. But notice the correspondence between the curvature of the backs of the heroes and of the sides of the vase and how, if they weren't bending over, we are to assume, their heads, especially Achilles' on the left, would pop out of the frame. This fact is an exclusive concern of *ours*, the real-world purveyors of the superior artistry of the vase, rather than of the heroes themselves, who exist in a dimension other than our own. That's the discourse.

By focusing exclusively on the future tense of the verb as the device *par excellence* of temporal artistry, then, Steiner limits himself to story and disregards discourse. I submit that the sort of syntactic artistry we've been considering today—and then only the first one and one-sixth lines of the 27,000+ lines of the *Iliad* and *Odyssey*—compensates for this oversight and provides a means by which the poet may engage in future-oriented artistry on the level of discourse to complement that on the level of story. And it's this neglect of temporal discourse as revealed through syntactic means, whose effect on the audience we've compared with the

---

[93] See page 97.

way music works on *its* audience, that results in translations that equate syntactically charged **menin** with syntactically flattened "anger" and seduce us into accepting such translations as acceptable simulacra of the so-called dead language of Homer.

Are translations enough? If there's one common thread throughout the theoretical literature on translation it's the fact that the notion that one can translate a work and capture all of its essentials, all of what one needs to become familiar with in order to be able to claim to really know a work of literature, is an illusion one clings to to compensate for believing in the superfluity of bothering to learn, of taking the time and putting in the effort to become familiar with, the language in its own terms. Granted, by doing so one encounters yet another obstacle which theorists like Derrida have addressed thoroughly and that is that even when we encounter works in the original language, our interpretation of texts are equally hampered by the idiosyncratic filters we see through. And yet one cannot deny that despite the text in its original language being no more semantically transparent than its approximations through translation, we at least have the advantage of initiating our inquiry on a level playing-field with the actual works passed down to us through the manuscript tradition of a given author.

Thus, far from a dead language, the language of Homer is so alive that we have to actually know it, rather than merely a paraphrase of it, to gain access to what's most, well, Homeric about it. This goes as well for the language of Horace, of Plato, of Cicero, indeed of any ancient stylist: to encounter their own words is to bypass the translator, the filter he or she places over their words, the perceptual and conceptual screens through which the words of the poet and the images they invoke are seen. To learn the Classics is to eavesdrop on the very origins of society, on conversations within the proto-Facebook of the *agora* and *forum*.

Aeschylus *Septem Quae Supersunt Tragoedias*, ed. Denys Page. Oxford Classical Texts (Oxford 1973).

Apollodorus *The Library*, 2 vols., ed. J.G. Frazer. Loeb Classical Library (Cambridge 1921).

Apollonius Rhodius *Argonautica*, ed. J. Fränkel. Oxford Classical Texts (Oxford 1986).

Apuleius *Metamorphoses*, ed. J.A. Hanson. Loeb Classical Library (Cambridge 1989-96).

Aristophanes *Comoediae*, 2 vols., ed. F.W. Hall, W.M. Geldart. Oxford Classical Texts (Oxford 1922).

Athenaios *Deipnosophistai*, 8 vols., ed. S.D. Olson. Loeb Classical Library (Cambridge 2012).

Callimachus *Hymns and Epigrams*, ed. A.W. Mair, G.R. Mair. Loeb Classical Library (Cambridge 1921).

Diodorus Siculus *Library of History*, ed. C.H. Oldfather, 3 vols. Loeb Classical Library (Cambridge, Mass. 1998-2000).

Dionysios of Halikarnassos *Roman Antiquities*, 7 vols., ed. E. Cary. Loeb Classical Library (Cambridge 1937-50).

Euripides *Fabulae,* 3 vols., ed. J. Diggle. Oxford Classical Texts (Oxford 1994).

Herodotus *The Persian Wars,* 4 vols., ed. A.D. Goldley. Loeb Classical Library (Cambridge 1920-25).

Hesiod *Theogony, Works and Days, Testimonia; The Shield, Catalogue of Women, Other Fragments*, 2 vols., ed. H. Evelyn-White. Loeb Classical Library (Cambridge 2007).

Homer *Opera*, 5 vols., ed. D.B. Monro, T.W. Allen. Oxford Classical Texts (Oxford 1920).

Homeric Hymns *Homeric Hymns Homeric Apocrypha Lives of Homer*, ed. M.L. West. Loeb Classical Library (Cambridge 2003).

Ovid *Metamorphoses*, ed. Roger A.B. Mynors. Oxford Classical Texts (Oxford 2004).

Pausanias *Pausanias' Description of Greece*, 6 vols., ed. J.G. Frazer, Loeb Classical Library (Cambridge 1898).

Pindar *Pindari Carmina cum Fragmentis*, ed. C.M. Bowra. Oxford Classical Texts (Oxford 1935).

Pliny *Natural History*, 10 vols., ed. B. Radice et al. Loeb Classical Library (Cambridge 1938-63).

Sophocles *Fabulae*, ed. H. Lloyd-Jones. Oxford Classical Texts (Oxford 1990).

Vergil *Opera*, ed. A.B. Mynors. Oxford Classical Texts (Oxford 1969).

119

E

Echo, 42
Edith Hamilton, 1
Egypt, 3, 6, 7, 8, 11, 23
Electra, 100
Electryon, 60, 61
Eleusis, 41, 43
Elysian Fields, 50
Enkidu, 10, 11, 12, 25
Ennead, 7
Eos, 14
Epic of Gilgamesh, 9, 10, 25
Erebos, 14
Eris, 84, 85
Eros, 14, 29
Ethiopia, 59
Eumenides, 100
Euripides, 46, 119
Eurystheus, 62, 64
Exekias, 96, 97, 117

F

Fertile Crescent, 9

G

Gaea, 5, 14, 15, 16, 17, 19, 29, 36
Geb, 5, 6
Gilgamesh, 9, 10, 11, 12, 25, 55, 61
Golden Fleece, 77, 78, 79
Gorgon, 31, 57, 67
Graeae, 50, 58

H

Hades, 7, 13, 16, 19, 30, 35, 41, 42, 44,
  50, 54, 58
Heaven, 20, 49, 50, 54
Hector, 96
Heinrich Schliemann, 83
Helen, 35, 84, 85, 99
Heliopolis Creation Myth, 4, 8, 9, 14,
  23

Helios, 14, 30, 43
Helius, 77
Hephaestus, 17, 19, 29, 33, 62, 72, 96
Hera, 16, 17, 19, 26, 27, 29, 33, 36, 41,
  44, 61, 62, 63, 68, 75, 84, 89
Heracles, 1, 2, 25, 27, 50, 57, 60, 61,
  62, 63, 64, 65, 67, 68, 69, 70, 71, 74,
  75, 76, 77, 78, 79, 81, 97
Hermes, 13, 19, 33, 44, 58, 59, 92
Hesiod, vi, 13, 16, 19, 119
Hesperides, 58
Hestia, 16, 19, 33, 34
Hierakonpolis, 3, 4
hieros gamos, 14
Hippodameia, 57
Homer, vi, 1, 2, 4, 13, 19, 20, 33, 76,
  81, 82, 88, 91, 103, 104, 108, 114,
  118, 119
Homeric Hymn to Hermes, 33
Homeric Question, 82
Horus, 4, 6, 7
Hyperion, 14

I

Iapetus, 14
Iliad, 2, 13, 19, 26, 29, 55, 62, 81, 82,
  83, 85, 87, 88, 90, 95, 103, 109, 111,
  114, 116, 117
Iolcus, 75
Ishtar, 11
Isis, 6, 7, 11
Ithaca, 51
Ithaka, 88, 89, 90, 92, 93, 106

J

Jason, 25, 75, 76, 77, 78, 79, 81

L

Laertes, 79, 88
Lapiths, 25
Leonidaion, 22
Lernean Hydra, 65

COMING IN 2016

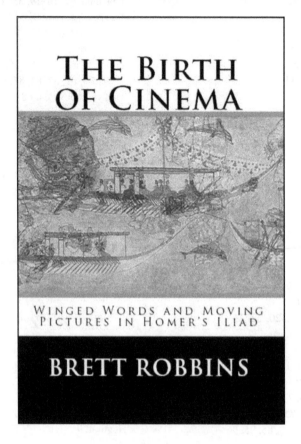

ABOUT THE AUTHOR

 Brett Robbins earned his Ph.D. in Classical Studies at Indiana University, Bloomington (dissertation [2004]: *Framing Achilles: Narrative Space in the Iliad*), and his B.A. and M.A. in Classics at University of California, Santa Barbara. He has traveled extensively, e.g., visiting over 100 ancient Greek sites with the American School of Classical Studies at Athens, delivering talks onsite at the Temple of Zeus at Olympia and the Theater of Epidaurus. He joined the Department of Classics and Humanities at San Diego State University in 2005, where he teaches courses in ancient Greek and Latin languages, myth, culture, etymology, drama, and cinema.

CPSIA information can be obtained
at www.ICGtesting.com
Printed in the USA
LVHW051933200722
723874LV00002B/280

9 780692 493205